M000204998

GIN

&

PHONICS

CLARA BATTEN

GIN & PHONICS

MY JOURNEY THROUGH MIDDLE-CLASS MOTHERHOOD (VIA THE OCCASIONAL PUB)

HarperCollins*Publishers*

HarperCollins*Publishers*
1 London Bridge Street
London SE1 9GF

www.harpercollins.co.uk

HarperCollins*Publishers*
Macken House, 39/40 Mayor Street Upper
Dublin 1, D01 C9W8, Ireland

First published by HarperCollins*Publishers* 2023

1 3 5 7 9 10 8 6 4 2

© Clara Batten 2023

Clara Batten asserts the moral right to
be identified as the author of this work

A catalogue record of this book is
available from the British Library

ISBN 978-0-00-850141-9

Printed and bound in the UK using 100%
renewable electricity at CPI Group (UK) Ltd

All rights reserved. No part of this publication may be
reproduced, stored in a retrieval system, or transmitted,
in any form or by any means, electronic, mechanical,
photocopying, recording or otherwise, without the
prior written permission of the publishers.

This book is produced from independently certified FSC™ paper
to ensure responsible forest management.

For more information visit: www.harpercollins.co.uk/green

This book is dedicated to my late father,
Howard, my mother, Louise, my two children,
Cressy and Monty, and my husband, Adam

CONTENTS

INTRODUCTION

Hello, you. I don't mean to sound like some Hugh Grant character in a Richard Curtis romcom, I'm literally saying hello. Because, if I'm honest, I never, not in a million years, thought I'd be here. Writing this book. Writing to you. Someone I've never met. I'm sure I'd want to meet you, given you've bought my book … Sh*t, I'm not saying that because I'm making money from you. What I mean is, the fact that you have an interest in buying this book probably means we are somewhat alike in many respects. Jeez, not just an 'interest' in buying this, you've given your own, hard-earned money over in exchange for it. Well, hopefully, it *was* your own money. I suppose you might have nicked it. And I have zero idea if you worked hard for it or not. Ahem, this has started out well … Last, but not least, hello to all the people who follow my ridiculous social media antics and want to see what the bloody hell I'm doing here.

Let me introduce myself. My name is Clara, but all my friends, family and even some of my old school teachers call me Ra. I'm 39. Yes, that's right, I will be the big 4–0 this year. In August, to be precise. I am married to Adam and we have two children: Cressida (Cressy), four, and Montgomery (Monty), almost three. We chose these names for our kids because we didn't want to reinforce any middle-class stereotypes. 👀

Some of you might know me from that really grown-up app, TikTok. To be honest, since the beginning of the pandemic, more grown-ups have started using it, but I can't pretend we are that grown-up on it. It's inadvertently become a big part of my life over the last two years, starting as a bit of escapism and then becoming a sort-of job, I suppose. I'll tell you all about how I came to be introduced to it a bit later – it's not at all embarrassing.

I bet you're wondering how this book came to be. No? Well, let me tell you anyway. So, when things became a bit more interesting in my life (and by 'interesting', I mean instead of Metanium nappy rash ointment being top of my shopping list, I began adding wigs and costumes for my online sketches), I set about writing down snapshots of my life, reflecting on all of those ridiculous and random things that happen when you're a parent and you begin sharing your life online, and, well, my weird life in general, and this book started to take shape.

One thing that, for me, falls into both the 'ridiculous' and 'random' categories is this little thing called phonics, which takes the alphabet as we all know it and turns it into a trainwreck of letters, which is then used as the basis of how kids are taught to read in primary schools. When Cressy started school and I discovered this system, my mind was so utterly blown (more on that later) that I decided this book would be structured around this word soup for no other reason than, well, it seemed like a nice idea at the time and also puns conveniently with my number-one love: a crisp, cold G&T. Maybe, just maybe, you've picked up this book because you're equally interested in this bastardisation of the traditional alphabet.

But even if you're not, don't bloody stop reading.

'S' IS FOR 'SCHOOL' ...

Aside from my kids' entry into the weird and wonderful world of primary schools, I have my own memories by which to gauge these extraordinary places and, albeit a massive cliché, these years were some of the greatest and most memorable of my life. My best friend of 32 years, Pip (who I met at primary school when I was eight), and I often have this conversation about how no other years in education really compare to the very formative ones. Maybe it's because we were so young that we look back on them with such fondness, whether playing hide and seek in the arts block or climbing trees we weren't meant to. Being sent to the headmaster's office. Going to the so-called haunted squash courts after school to scare ourselves sh*tless. Counting every tiny little Nerd while sharing them out between the two of us at break time (the sweets I mean, not the boringly studious kids ... that would be *too* weird). Lifting the lids of our old-fashioned wooden desks to check for love letters first thing in the morning. Swimming in the pool on speech day when there was no supervision. Being sent to the headmaster's office. Playing conkers and marbles (which isn't really allowed now because of health and safety). Being separated in our French lesson for giggling and being told to face each back corner of the room, which made us giggle more uncontrollably. Being sent to the headmaster's office. Calling 192 directory enquiries from the school payphone as it was 'free', asking for weird numbers in strange accents and finding it so funny, we hung up … Until one day when they called back and threatened to call the police. Wait, what? That last one was a joke, obviously.

The teachers nicknamed Pip and I 'The Terrible Twins' and, now I've written it down in black and white, I can see they were utterly justified. We weren't arseholes, just – as I like to put it – kids with personalities. We liked to get up to mischief. But we were never nasty and always wanted others to feel included and happy (which inevitably got them in trouble as well), but at no time were we disrespectful. OK, maybe very occasionally to the 192 operator. Joking … That whole prank call thing was totally fabricated, OK? Didn't happen.

All of us remember the little things at our primary school. I remember the smell in the corridors, having my make-up done for school plays in the dining room while eating rock cakes (which, incidentally, must have been made from actual rocks given that it took 36 minutes to eat one while trying not to chip a tooth). Spilling hot tea on my arm (I mean, who gives an eight-year-old tea, anyway?) and being told, in fact, that it was nothing a green wet paper towel couldn't sort out. But not a soft one. No, thank you. One that was akin to cardboard and felt like sandpaper. And for goodness' sake don't make the water on it cold, make sure it's lukewarm by the time you put it on my arm.

Fast forward 28 years and my daughter Cressy goes to a school like mine. The hallways look the same, the smell is similar, the laughter as kids run through the corridors and slow down when they see a teacher identical; the big oak trees lining the driveway ... She even has the same chocolate sponge squares with anaemic chocolate sauce which is less like a sauce and more like normal custard which once had a minor fling with some chocolate powder. It's still my favourite pudding even though I've not eaten it for 23 years. I asked Cressy if she could sneak me out a square with some sauce on it next time she has it. She asked why her brother couldn't do it. Well, for one thing, Monty goes to a nursery which is at a different school to the one Cressy is at. Although that wouldn't really matter as I'm 100 per cent certain he too has these chocolate puddings. I decide that his age is the issue here.

'Monty is only just about to turn three.'

'And I'm only four. So how am I going to get the chocolate sauce out? I can't wrap it in tissue like the cake.'

'Yes, quite. Sorry, I've not thought this through.'

*   *   *

Cressy is learning all sorts of things at school – Maths, English, even the odd bit of French. She has music lessons and swimming lessons and, well, phonics. This should be the most basic thing for me to comprehend (because, you know, they're teaching it to four-year-olds) but I won't deny that I've found it difficult to wrap my head around. Look, I get it. At least I get the concept. I sort of get why they do it … It even kind of makes sense. No, I'm lying, I don't get it at all.

I first heard of phonics when my 10-year-old niece Isla started reception. I was reading with her and I said, 'This starts with a "B" as you would say to an adult. Like "bee".' She said, 'Well, it's a "buh" but yes.' Sorry, what? My brother, Ben ('Buh'-en), explained to me that this was correct and that they now teach phonics rather than the old school alphabet. Sorry, what?!

The other day we got invited to a parents' evening, where the teachers gave us an induction into how, what and why they teach phonics. I was half-annoyed at what I was about to hear and half utterly intrigued by what could possibly be any school's justification for not teaching actual letters of the alphabet. Ten minutes in and I couldn't help but glance around the room to scope out what other parents might be thinking. And although there were some concrete nods of approval, I singled out two and a half people who looked on my wavelength of slight ambiguity about the whole thing. Was anyone going to be brave enough to question further, or were we all, very Britishly, going to sit there and bob our heads in time to the speech?

One father put up his hand and asked, 'So, when did this method of teaching come about? When I was at school we learnt the letters as the normal alphabet. You know, so they knew the actual letters and how they were pronounced.' *Thank you*. He took the words right out of my mouth; the words I wasn't actually going to say because, well, I was too scared but also slightly relieved that for once, I wasn't THAT parent.

The teacher said, 'Oh, it's always been around.' B*llocks! OK, sounding letters has always been a thing, but there was DEFINITELY a time when the board of something or other decided this method was going to be the one used in the official curriculum. There was a time when all schools got on board with this way of teaching and thought it would be better than the hundreds of years spent teaching it the other way. And that blows my mind. Were they like, 'Um, did you see that school has started not teaching the alphabet as we know it? They are literally saying how it sounds but not what the letter actually is?' And then the other school said, 'Yeah, but that's ridiculous. No way will they get anyone else to do it. I mean, it's really bad teaching; basically, saying a completely different way of sounding 26 letters which, singularly, you will never hear pronounced like that ever in your life again, because, well, they are not the letters. Hang on … Holy sh*t, look, *five* other schools have started doing it. Maybe we should too, what do you think?'

'Are you out of your mind? They're four years old, not 18 months.'

At least that's how I reckon it went anyway. Skip forward a year and everyone is talking to four-year-old kids at school like they're just out of the womb.

But IT WORKS somehow. I have to trust the process. What these teachers are telling me is proven, or they wouldn't do it surely? In all seriousness, it makes sense. It makes perfect sense. But it's just odd that this is now the thing. The way. But yes, I'm obviously still struggling with it a little. I mean, the word 'phonics' doesn't even begin with an 'F' phor ph*ck's sake …

Cressy arrived home with her book bag with a reading book in it and another small book inside labelled 'Notes from teacher to parent and parent to teacher'.

'What's this?' I ask.

'My homework.'

Um, sorry? I thought I had at least a couple of years before this starts and now it seems I have homework too. I need to get on board with this. After all, Cressy seems incredibly enthusiastic and I should at least be grateful for that. We sit down to read. It's a very thin book. This is going to be quick and painless, I think. I turn the page to begin and see a picture, so I say, 'That's nice, let's turn to the next page and find some words to read.'

'Oh no, Mummy, there are no words,' Cressy replies.

Hang on a bl**dy second. At this point I'm not sure if I'm elated by the prospect of how easy this is going to be and how little time it's going to take, or furious that the teachers have played some kind of sick joke on me. Or, if they haven't played a joke, I could be enraged that we're now paying through the nose for our daughter to ultimately look at pictures in a book after we've just had a talk at the school on how phonics is an absolute necessity when learning to read. This school is quite prestigious, there must be reasoning behind this 'method'. I make a mental note to look this up when the kids are asleep, then leave it there and continue through the book, which is akin to those I read to Cressy when she was 10 months old, but actually less complicated as there were actual words in those books and at least some touchy-feely sensory elements to them, which I find myself praying for on the next page to make it a bit more interesting. At least as far as I'm concerned anyway.

I'm talking (as it tells me to do on the cover of the book) about everything that's going on in each picture. My worry is though that I have no idea what IS actually going on. Luckily for me, Cressy informs me that she knows as they have 'read this book' at school today ... TWICE. WTAF? So, let me get this straight. My four-year-old is learning to read by sounding out letters, but not *learning* the letters, reading books with no words and then being sent home to do homework, which entails looking at the same pictures she has already looked at twice today to try and figure out what's going on in the story, which she has also completed and talked about two times today already?

At least she's having a good time talking through each picture and weirdly this very basic book has got me a bit hooked on what's going to happen next. Once Cressy points out that the dog isn't just standing in the garden looking gormlessly into the sky, but is in fact looking for the ball which is actually behind the tyre, it becomes something of a suspense novel. A novel without words.

I write in the feedback book, 'Cressy did very well describing the pictures in the book, which was surprising as she informed me she had only talked about each page in the book twice today. Bravo, Cressy.' Looking back at it 45 seconds later, it may have been a little too sarcastic for a parent report going straight into the teacher's hands in the morning, but I've had quite a bit of 'banter' with her teachers at the school gates before so I feel I might get away with it, while giving them a nudge that they may need to explain more about why this technique is so great. I could just ask them rather than put something in the written word like I'm writing a comedy sketch which could easily be misconstrued as rude or passive aggressive. I think better of it and use a rubber for the first time in 23 years. It's almost as if I knew I was going to be a tw*t when I picked up a pencil and not a pen to write the feedback.

I came downstairs and immediately left a voice note for Pip, who is now a primary school teacher, to ask whether this is in fact a thing. She told me that it is indeed something they do, in order to encourage kids to talk about and describe what they are seeing, almost to tell their own story in a descriptive way and by talking WITH you about it and talking about what they think the letter is that the object begins with and how the boy or the dog is feeling (which I definitely did, by the way). Apparently, it gets their creativity going. She DID say, though, that this part is not to do with phonics as such. Or, at all really.

Now she's said that I feel better – that, firstly, I'm not going mad and this is a definite thing and we're not being taken the p*ss out of, and, secondly, that it's also actually a really great way of getting the kids to be creative. So, I applaud you, my child's school. What a 180! Pip called me very soon after our WhatsApp liaison to remind me of a phonics story she had about teaching that's just too good not to share.

When teaching her Year 2s phonics, she had told them about the fact that the 'o' and 'u' letters together didn't always mean you sounded them as 'ow' but sometimes as 'ŭ'. When a pupil questioned her on an example, she said, 'Like "country". We don't say country as "cowntry" and we also don't write country as …' And just as she'd turned to the whiteboard and written, in big letters, c … u … n … t … the headmaster walked in, showing prospective parents around. She didn't want to appear rude by carrying on writing but she also didn't want to bring attention to the board (which would have also been rude in an entirely different way), so she stepped away from it and decided chatting to them was the best method of distraction, all the while having the word 'c*nt' written in plain sight of

20 children, a headmaster and a set of prospective parents, in large letters across the board. I couldn't have her end the story there so I asked if she got away with it.

'Yeah, of course. If you call the parents squinting at the whiteboard and then raising their eyebrows in disbelief 'getting away with it', and then the headmaster asking me if he could have a word in his office at break time after the parents left the classroom, then yeah, totally nailed covering that gem up.'

*　　*　　*

After my initial shock at discovering our daughter wouldn't be learning to read using the alphabet had dissipated, I decided to look up a few things regarding phonics. The first thing I wanted to know was when this took over from the standard A, B, Cs we learnt at school. Naturally, I google 'When did teaching phonics begin?'

The first result that comes up is, 'Phonics is not new. It began to be used after 1850.' EIGHTEEN-FIFTY. Are you having a laugh? Sometimes I think Google is just trying to p*ss me off. I'm sure there's some dickhead inside my Google being like, 'Nah, don't give her that. That's true. Didn't you hear what she said? She doesn't believe phonics has been going that long. Let's have a bit of fun …'

I stick with the first page of results and after one swipe up of my finger, I scroll to something that really piques my interest: 'How phonics took over when teaching children to read in primary schools.' A quick skim and I can already see within the article the numbers 1997. That's more like it.

Now, I'm going to quote a few parts of this article by the *Economist* in 2019 because I don't believe there aren't more parents out there who would also like to know more about why, how and where this phonics sorcery began. But I'm genuinely intrigued, because although I joked above about how I reckon it all started, it would be good to know who led the movements and what the science behind it all is. OK, go!

It looks like phonics was starting to be talked about a couple of years before I left school at 18. The conversations really began in 1997, which makes perfect sense as I don't remember hearing anything of this when I was at school. And to be honest, I wouldn't have heard about it anyway, even if it had started to be taught at my school, as I'm pretty sure I had learnt to read by the time I was 16 when these conversations were in full force.

The article states: '*Labour began to promote phonics after it came to power in 1997. Mr Gibb, who became schools minister under the Tory–Lib Dem coalition in 2010, then upped the emphasis. The curriculum was tweaked, and funding set aside for textbooks and training.*'

By the way, stop me if this is getting at all boring for you. Oh no, wait, you can't. I'll have to carry on. But I'm truly fascinated. Having to start a whole new way of teaching from scratch is no mean feat. Talking as if I know. You know when I had to completely change the whole

Maths curriculum back in 2008, it was one of the hardest things I've ever had to do.

No, I didn't. I've never done anything of the sort. Not even got close to touching a textbook since leaving school.

But seriously, I can imagine it takes a lot of hard work and dedication – the time and effort in changing a curriculum so dramatically. New teacher training courses, new textbooks, new activities to focus on, new worksheets, new games to teach through and new YouTube videos to source. OK, that last one's pretty easy. But you know, you're effectively changing a whole structure of teaching one of the most fundamental parts of any child's life, learning to read.

The article goes on to talk about how teachers have been split on their thoughts and views as to whether phonics is a better way to teach in comparison to the 'old way' of teaching. Yep, thought as much …

'Teachers have long argued about whether this approach is better than the previously favoured one, in which children learned to recognise whole words, typically while someone reads to them. To critics there is something Gradgrindian about phonics, which they argue fails to transmit the joy of reading.'

I had to look up 'Gradgrindian' (well, I asked Google on my smart speaker while I sat on my arse, physically looking up nothing). I had to ask to know what the hell this last sentence meant. Google says: *Having a soulless devotion to facts and figures; inflexibly utilitarian. adjective.* Yep, still no clue …

So, what's a *soulless devotion to facts and figures*? I don't actually care, but I do know Gradgrindian is my new favourite word and I will be using it at any time it's even the slightest, tiniest bit relevant. Because there's not a hope in hell that anyone, even if they've heard the word before, will know what it means. I think I need to go back to school. I've already got a new thirst for knowledge – and not even in an intellectual or swotty way, that's just not in my DNA. But maybe because I'm writing words down rather than getting the kids ready for school, or clearing up a child's sick, or singing them to sleep or putting washing in the dryer. A part of my brain is suddenly being utilised again and I'm quite liking it.

Anyway, I digress ... I was saying how much the kids respond to this way of teaching. Or was I? Well, I was at least going to go ON to that.

The article continues: '*The shift in teaching methods reflects both persuasive evidence and political pressure. In 2005 a study in Scotland found that children who were taught using phonics were, by the end of the programme, seven months ahead of their expected reading and spelling ability. Rebecca Allen of the University of Oxford notes that few teaching methods are backed by such strong evidence.*'

Surely you can't argue with that. Actual studies. Proven science..

And, '*The impact is becoming apparent. England's performance improved in the latest Progress in International Reading Literacy Study, a cross-country comparison.*'

And despite the fact that some teachers remain unconvinced by the change, the article says, '*over the past decade or so schools in England have adopted the method. When Nick Gibb, a minister, declared the "debate is over" earlier this year, in 2019, disagreement was muted.*'

Not totally sure about the 'muted' thing but I suppose these conversations would go on for years if not and everyone has to get on with it. So here we are and there we have it. Reading what I have, along with how the teachers have described the benefits of phonics, my mind has officially been changed to being completely behind phonics as a method of teaching. Being taught sounds of letters so children can read by sounding the word out per letter has to be more useful than being taught to recognise whole words. And indeed, it is. I bet you're so pleased that I, a woman with no teaching experience, has given phonics her backing.

You're welcome.

'A' IS FOR 'ACTING' ...

As you might have guessed from my complete and unwavering devotion to the method by which our daughter learns to read, I am a girl (I can't describe myself as 'woman' or 'lady' – one seems too old for how I feel, the other too prim and proper) who succumbed, in an excited way, to being a mum as my job, for, let's say, the foreseeable future.

This was genuinely exciting to me. It's something I had wished for since my mid-twenties. I was bored of partying, of living the London life. Don't get me wrong, I loved it, but I craved 'that other life'. The kids. The simplicity (simplicity with kids, what? You know what I mean). The family. The simplicity of family life. Again, not really a thing. The simple life? Um, nope. OK ... So, maybe, just not the rat race, working 9–6 every day, commuting, eating, drinking, bed. Repeat. I genuinely couldn't wait to be a mum and experience a completely new world of disorientation, chaos and love.

But what made me really want to write this book – and it's hard, and daunting, knowing I'll eventually write

70,000 words – is that I want to show you can pursue things you're passionate about, things you really want to get off the ground, while also being a parent. And, during the process (as I'll ably demonstrate), you will get some pretty incredible, sometimes humorous, but often quite mediocre anecdotes along the way.

But seriously, I think it's quite easy to believe that we can't give our all to both parenting *and* work and therefore we're doomed to fail at both. This is certainly how I felt when I stopped work at eight months pregnant with my first. I knew that in the job I was in, there was going to be little flexibility when it came to going back part-time or leaving early to collect a child from nursery, and therefore I would either need wraparound childcare and hardly ever see my very young child, paying my entire pay cheque to the nursery or childminder, or not go back to work and become a full-time mother until they were both at school at almost five years old (and then still pay for after-school clubs to get them to 5 p.m., which would still mean leaving work early to collect them).

I've heard a lot of people say they feel this way and, seriously, I don't know how ANYONE does it. In the grand scheme of things, and although stuff hasn't always been easy financially, I know I was fortunate to be able to make the choice to step away from formal work for the first few years. Some might say this is the opposite of fortunate, given the chaos of early years' parenting. Once, Adam came in from work and said, 'Bloody hell, what a day! I had two massive meetings back-to-back. I didn't even get to have lunch until 3 p.m. How was your day, did you just have a chilled one?'

'Yes. Yes, I did. If "chilled" is walking a 20-month-old – who is in the middle of potty training – and a newborn to the park, with the newborn screaming for my knockers on a busy road in London, me flustered in 29-degree heat, sitting on someone's front wall, trying to get a boob out, while also holding my leg out in front of our toddler so she doesn't go near the road, her then lying down on the pavement, having a tantrum because we still weren't at the park and then complaining the concrete she is lying on is too hot on her back. Then me begging her, through tears, to please stand up while I'm attempting to burp a refluxy baby. All the while, a sweet older gentleman notices my struggle from the other side of the road and rushes over to help, only to be greeted by Cressy clasping onto the wheel of the buggy, legs in the air, with no knickers on so that the man then made a quick detour back to where he came from, muttering "sorry" just in case I accused him of being a paedo probably. Then, yes, it was really chilled.

'Good news is though, I managed to pull Cressy off the ground and, as I did, I was holding onto Monty so firmly, he eventually burped and was sick all over Cressy's face. So every cloud ... But at least I've eaten. I had a delicious babies' rusk biscuit, two of Cressy's Quavers and three sips of an iced coffee before Monty whacked it out of my hand onto the windscreen of a black BMW.'

It was days like these (and they weren't all like this, obviously) when I sometimes wished for the 'different simplicity' of going back into the office. You know, brushing my hair in the morning, having grown-up chats, laughing with people who didn't think that the word 'poo' was the height of comedic entertainment ... oh, and doing some work, of course.

There definitely comes a time though when we all, no matter what we say, become a teensy bit competitive with our partners once kids are around with regards to the 'who has it worse' scenario, from work to sleep deprivation. This isn't a 'serious' thing, by the way. OK, maybe it's a little bit serious, but I do find it bloody funny. I'm sure I'm not the only one, but my husband Adam (more so back then) is completely unaware of what actually goes on in a standard day or night of a stay-at-home parent. One morning he woke up and said, 'I feel so tired today, did you hear that siren at about 1 a.m.? And I'm even more pissed off that I woke up 25 minutes before my alarm went off and couldn't get back to sleep.'

I said, 'God, that must have been exhausting. I hope today is going to be OK for you. I feel alright, as I only got up twice to feed, burp and change the baby, who had a nappy full of wet sh*t, which had leaked all over his sleep sack. And only got up one more time to comfort Cressy back to sleep after she had a nightmare, before getting up with them at 6.30 a.m., which incidentally is 45 minutes before your alarm goes off.'

OK, so maybe this 'competition' is more of a one-sided thing.

'Really? Wow, I didn't hear a thing.'

I don't want to 'sleep like a baby', I want to sleep like my husband.

*   *   *

Now, where were we? Oh yes, 'A' is for 'Acting' ...

Growing up, my parents would tell me to do whatever made me happy. And I'm sure my careers adviser at school was absolutely over the moon both at my parents supporting me in wanting to go into one of the most competitive industries there is and the fact that I enthusiastically stated, at 14 years old, 'I want to be an actress.' I remember one career adviser looking at me through slightly disbelieving eyes and saying, 'OK, and as a backup?'

'Nothing, thanks.'

'But, Clara, acting is very difficult to get into and earn a living from, so it's good to have something else on your radar.'

'Oh, I see,' I said. 'Sure. Well, I'm coming up to Grade 8 in ballet, modern and jazz dancing and if that's not a goer, singing would be my third choice.' As she nodded slowly, I could see her passion for the chat waning. I mean, what person being paid to talk very seriously about career options doesn't want to hear, 'Acting, singing and dancing, please' as someone's only choices, as if there was no doubt they were going to be the next big hit on the West End stage? I remember saying in a jokingly sarcastic tone, 'What do you want me to say, that I want to be a doctor, vet or astronaut, like I said when I was five?'

'Well, yes.'

But my mother was always behind me. And thank God she was, as I then spent countless years living it up in London, getting very close to auditions, not earning a living on stage or screen, having some decidedly non-acting jobs in the meantime, working in bars and restaurants in the evenings, underpaid, with antisocial hours, and scraping by at the end of the month. It was just how I'd always imagined the actor's life. And to that careers adviser: see, I told you I'd make it. If you've seen it, the film *Withnail and I* sums up the out-of-work actor's life perfectly, although looking back on it now, maybe watching the film for the 26th time while trying to be an actor probably wasn't the greatest motivation. And taking on board any of their extra-curricular activities from the film probably even more of a hindrance. I did not do any of these things, I swear.

Honestly, though, I don't regret a thing, partly because of that constant support from my mum, which allowed me to pursue the dream and gave me licence to push to do so without feeling the pressure of hearing 'I told you so' if it didn't work out. And if there's one thing it has done, it has kept the fire in my belly alive that I STILL will – it has honestly never left me. That's not to say that if you don't have supportive parents, you can't pursue your dreams.

Pursue them no matter what and you too could have 15 years' experience of hammering phones in cold call centres while you wait for the next call from your agent who you didn't know had retired before you accidentally saw him on *Who Wants to Be a Millionaire?* while working behind a bar in Putney. Um, that didn't happen to me ...

But long story short, although I got an acting agent and moved to London when I was 18, it never quite worked out the way I thought it would. Saying that, one highlight of my acting career sticks out. Back then, I had not only joined my 'proper' acting agent but also been taken on by an 'extras agency' for 'extra' roles and walk-on parts. I didn't tell my proper agent though as joining an extras agency was unprofessional as a serious actor and a complete no-no. But I had heard that sometimes they auditioned people from the extras agencies for small parts in TV and film. Even if I wasn't going to get one of these parts, at least if I was an extra, I was going to be working in the industry at times on a real-life set. Even if it was walking into the loo in the background of a busy hospital on *Casualty* for £80 a day ...

So anyway, the highlight of my career back then ... I got a part in *EastEnders*. A proper speaking part with lines. I was one of three actors in the scene: me, Pauline and Pat. Now that was incredible. I had three small lines to learn but I had them nailed. It was a flashback episode to when they first met and they were having an argument on the bus. I had to say something like, 'Come on, ladies. Stop that, we're all grown-ups.' Although I remember the director saying, 'The line is "Oi, girls. THAT'S ENOUGH. Get off her!" and if you could say it less Surrey, more cockney …' Anyway, I'm very pleased to say, when we all sat down to watch it at home, half of one line I said was kept in the scene, but the whole of my back was shown. Don't get jealous.

A couple of months went by and I received a phone call. I didn't recognise the number at first as I had got a new phone and also I hadn't heard from this person in … well, forever. It was my proper agent (who hadn't yet retired, of course). I couldn't believe it. He said, 'You've got a part. And you don't need to audition! They want you.' He sounded very pleased with himself.

'Oh my God, what is it? This is AMAZING!'

'It's at the start of a new detective series.'

'I LOVE detective dramas!' I announced.

'A body is washed up on the beach and is found early in the morning by a policewoman,' he told me.

'Gritty! Yes?'

'And you would be the body.'

FFS.

Needless to say, my late teens and early twenties were not quite going according to plan. And although I got the odd day of work here and there, my day job in media sales (cold calling, selling advertising space to me and you) or my night job working in a bar seemed so often to be my destiny. It was a little deflating to say the least but also, being in my late teens/twenties in arguably the best city in the world, I probably didn't do EVERYTHING I could towards giving it a shot because I was too busy loving life. I wasn't knocking on directors' doors. I wasn't sending my acting CV out, left, right and centre. I do remember, though, looking through the book *Contacts* – a holy grail for actors – and writing personally to the new casting director of *EastEnders*. OK, looking back on this now, either I had an unhealthy obsession with *EastEnders*, or I didn't realise anything else was actually on TV at the time. But I HAD to write to the casting director, because someone p*ssed in the bar I worked in the night before had said I would make a great 'Saskia', the posh bird in *EastEnders* who died when nightclub owner Steve Owen embedded a marble ashtray into her skull. I mean, if a bloke seven pints in and two tequila shots down didn't know what he was talking about, who did?! And after my very detailed letter to the casting director, explaining how much some random person I had never met before thought of me, omitting the small point of how much he had drunk, I was somewhat surprised not to have been offered an audition at least.

Anyway, I digress. My point being, we are often too young (and I don't mean this in a patronising way) to take on board where we want to be and how to do it. Of course, so much in life is a game of luck. It is, and I appreciate that. You meet the right people. You fall into the right hands but you can also make your own destiny and I have found this more as I have got older. Way more. And way older.

I have seen many, many friends, family, acquaintances and people on social media I don't know succeed more now that they are parents than what they perceived as being successful in their youth, working tirelessly for someone in a 'mediocre' job in comparison to what they actually wanted to do and are doing now. Lots of my friends have done the same. They've got to their mid-thirties and thought, no. They've started up their own businesses or re-trained online. And these aren't just parents, some are single friends who just happen to be having proper midlife crises like me.

What I do online – create absolutely bloody hysterical videos (ahem) on TikTok – is not classed as 'a real job'. I've been told this often by people online. Negative people who I don't give a sh*t about, frankly. And I think it's because things which are deemed as creative, fun and enjoyable can't possibly be labelled 'work'. And, in a way, they're right. As the old saying by Mark Twain goes, 'Find a job you enjoy doing, and you will never have to work a day in your life.' Which reminds me of one of my favourite quotes from Cressy. In fact, I might have to sprinkle some Cressy quotes throughout this book – they shall be called 'Quotes by Cressy'.

Original.

QUOTES BY CRESSY

Me: 'What do you want to be when you grow up?'

Cressy: 'A doctor and a mummy.'

Me: 'Oh, that's lovely, Cressy. You don't want to be an actor anymore?'

Cressy: 'Oh, I love acting. I will always do that. But it's not really a JOB though, is it, Mummy?'

In between laughing, I managed to let her know that when something is really enjoyable, it doesn't feel like work. I should probably just stay quiet and enjoy the fact she mentioned two very worthwhile and respectable jobs rather than continue to talk up the most unreliable career one could pick. But I spend a lot of time doing my 'non-real' TikTok job and it takes time and effort. Way more than I'd like most of the time. Like, two hours for a one-minute sketch, often for only a few thousand views. At least I can earn about 2.1p from a video like that. But you're writing sketches, acting them out, playing loads of characters, creating adverts for brands, doing parody songs, vlogging, documenting charity work, doing silly comedy dances (I mean, writing this down in real life, it's not actually sounding the most attractive of job prospects). That said, I get to do it from home, around being a mum. Reliving my passion while having a three- and four-year-old, but still playing with them, doing puzzles with them, watching movies with them, reading to them; have a job, while having kids, do school pickups, go out for lunch or a coffee in the middle of the day, take half terms off and be happy. Almost all of the time. OK, just most of the time, which is still a lot.

I took a shot at social media, something I'd only really used as a means to post photos of nights out or the food I had cooked, and it was only on one site – I'm not sure if you'll remember it, Facebook or something. But by throwing myself into two other sites – TikTok and Instagram – and thanks to some handy pieces of publicity along the way, I got bigger than I ever thought I'd be (but that was more the drinking and stuffing my face during lockdown). Anyway, I also became a bit bigger on social media. I absolutely love this medium for getting your stuff out there, but I'm still pursuing my acting dreams, (I can hear you saying, 'WHAT? Maybe don't. I'm not sure you remember the few anecdotes you just told us about trying to be an actor …') Well, I'm going to screw with your mind some more now. I'm still pursuing my TV scriptwriting dreams too and I'm about to embark on co-writing a film. The only actual thing I've succeeded at so far though in the creative industry is that I'm now a published bloody author. Never going to get used to that. But I'm so fortunate to have the opportunity to write this book. So lucky to be able to share a section of my life with you. YOU may not feel so lucky by the end, mind.

It all came about as I was doing what makes me happy – performing and working quite hard at it. If someone had told me when I was 12 that at 39, I would land a book deal for performing, I would have thought, 'Wow, I'm going to be a big Hollywood star, writing my memoirs.' Instead, it's, 'I can be quite funny doing some videos in my home during a global pandemic and gain a few followers on a thing called social media, and some guy who worked in publishing happened across my page because a celebrity he actually wanted to talk to mentioned me somewhere.' I like to think of it as sort of the same thing though, right?

So, one day, someone appeared on my TikTok livestream 'saying' they were from HarperCollins. At first I thought that it must be someone mucking around, but then I thought, no, how else would a senior executive publisher from one of the most renowned publishing companies in the world get in touch if it isn't on TikTok at 11 p.m.? If I'm honest, I secretly hoped he wasn't lying but I was a little p*ssed at the time. It was a Friday night and I was being my usual crazy self. You know, kids in bed, husband in his office and me on TikTok, all by myself, gin and tonic in hand, and, as the MailOnline might say, flaunting my curves in PJ bottoms and slipper socks. I just happened to be dancing, talking to a load of strangers and potentially slurring my words. I know, you wish you had my life ... I didn't think to write down his name to message or email him, so I asked him to DM (that's direct message – I might use this abbreviation a lot in this book) me on yet another social media platform, Instagram.

Obviously, given the way DMs work, this was lost among many others in the spam folder. Fast forward a fortnight and I saw that he had messaged me. So why the hell did he get in touch? Long story short:

1. Jeremy Clarkson wrote a piece in *The Sun* newspaper slagging off the BBC (he never does this … I was in total shock too) but complimenting ME (thank you, Jez). I can't quite remember what the exact words were. It was something like, 'She is to my mind, what Joe Wicks is to your body.' Oh, turns out I can. How odd.

2. A publisher at HarperCollins was having a call with Jezza Clarkson (I feel we are at that stage now, where we can have nicknames for each other) so read the recent article he wrote and then started following me. Not in a creepy way. Just on social media, although that can be quite creepy sometimes too.

3. He liked my humour and decided that a punt on someone who was quite comedic but had never written anything close to a book before, and in fact had little time to read anything herself, might be a good business decision.

4. I had an actual 'old-fashioned' phone call with him. He said, 'OK, so if you write about 3,000 words in the next two weeks and send it across, I can talk to the team and we could maybe make you an offer.'

Wait. What?

So here I am. I started writing this book as soon as I got off the phone. A whole paragraph of about 34 words. Yep, 34 words. Move over, Dawn French. No, please don't.

It's really daunting, but he said, 'Write how you would talk.'

So, I am. Probably too much, in fact. And I haven't even started properly yet.

Hang on. FIGHT. I'm not propositioning you, I'm just standing between my kids. Monty's about to bite Cressy for taking all the red Lego. Sorry, what was that? You're not meant to write a book on your phone, while standing in the middle of a preschool argument halfway through your second large glass of wine?

Pedantic.

You're going to hear some funny and probably quite literally sh*tty stories on motherhood – I am a mum after all – but I want the mum thing to be incidental, not what defines this or me. I'm really hoping to show some sort of growth, both personally as a parent and wife (yeah, I mean, we'll take that one with a pinch of salt), but also professionally, since deciding quite recently to give my all once more towards a passion I have never quite let go of:

acting. However, if by the end of this 12–18 months I'm in the exact same place as where I started, at least I've written a sodding book explaining in depth exactly how to get no further along in life and, more importantly, how much work you need to put in, in order to achieve this.

LIFE LESSON ACCORDING TO CLARA BATTEN: 1

MOTHERHOOD IS A COMMA, NOT A FULL STOP.

That is to say, so many people I know (myself included) have started the careers they always dreamed of after having children. Let's hope this acting thing works out, otherwise I might have to backtrack on this one.

'T' IS FOR 'TIKTOK' ...

Even if you're not 13 watching dance trend tutorials in your bedroom, you probably know what TikTok is. Because it has grown to be so much more than that. Really. In fact, Jezza (Clarkson) explains the concept far better than I do ...

'It's bite-sized clips from comedy classics like *Blackadder*, it's bits of Joe Biden introducing himself as "Joe Biden's brother", it's great goals, and Formula One crashes and Jimmy Carr and air show highlights and dogs falling over and yes, occasionally, girls in bikinis miming to Ariana Grande and totally original content too, and trends, but;

'You watch one thing and you have no idea what's coming up next. It's like being blindfolded then dipping your hand into a box of chocolates that an algorithm has filled with only stuff it knows you'll like. And it's so addictive, there's even a feature to make you stop watching after 90 minutes.'

I actually feel very lucky that TikTok is something good to have come out of the pandemic for me and it has also opened doors for which I am extremely grateful. *Loose Women* first showed a TikTok of mine on their show when I was still relatively new to the app. They didn't bother telling me about it, but how very lucky I was to have stumbled across it one day, after searching countless 'On Demand' streams of the programme for an hour and a half, after a follower commented they had seen me on it. Then a few well-known people – including Peter Andre and Ulrika Jonsson – commented on my videos and shared them on social media. I was quick to point out to my husband that this would be really exciting if it was 1995. Still, I'm grateful – I'm not an arsehole. *LADbible* shared one of my videos, which got me a shed-load more followers within hours, and also *The Poke* and *Netmums*. Excuse me while I pick up a few names I've dropped. All this has been nothing but positive and, despite my bravado, I do feel very humbled.

The story of how I ended up with a TikTok account begins with my husband Adam. It was his fault. Or fault-lessness. A dance routine to the song 'Blinding Lights' was trending. All the NHS workers were doing it and upload-ing videos online because they were a bit bored and didn't have much to do, being on the frontline during a global pandemic and all that.

Anyway, Adam showed me a few versions of the dance and said, 'You know me, I'm not into social media but I literally downloaded TikTok purely to watch people doing this dance. Not in a weird way. And don't tell anyone. Nonetheless, I think you could do this dance.'

Challenge accepted. Oh, and Adam, your secret is safe with me.

I mean, I don't wish to brag or anything, but as you know, between the ages of five and 15, I did quite a few grades of ballet, modern and jazz dance (I bloody knew they would come in handy one day) so I had a sneaking suspicion I would absolutely nail it.

I pretended I was a little nervous at the prospect of learning such a high-profile social media dance which lasted 12 seconds, but secretly I was just looking forward to my husband's proud face and congratulations, given his unhealthy obsession with the dance.

Turns out, it was one of the most difficult things I have ever had to try to coordinate in my life. Who even thought this arm and leg combo would actually work? I mean, somehow it looks quite cool but everything about it is alien and I'm saying that with a background in what I, but no one else, would call 'semi-pro dancing'. The first leg crossing over the other while swiping the arms up in the opposite direction ... it's just wrong. When I fell over my own legs in what looked like the simplest of moves, I explained to Adam, who was patiently holding the phone ready to record, that maybe he should get on with some work as this dance had obviously been created by *Riverdance*'s Michael Flatley and I needed a bit of time to get up to speed.

And I did. An hour and a half to be precise, while my kids intermittently asked Mummy worriedly if she needed help in any way. But after 94 minutes, I had it down.

'OK, so you've practised enough that I won't need to stand here for loads of takes, yeah?' Adam asked.

'Yeah, sure. If you like.'

Seven takes later, out of breath, a frustrated Adam in tow, and my kids repeatedly asking, 'Is Mummy OK?', I had indeed nailed it.* I uploaded it to my newly created TikTok account, thinking I would caption it, 'One take wonder' but then thought better of it, as, firstly, I might be done under some sort of 'description act' and, secondly, 'I don't want to con my potential future fan base. We can't start our relationship off on a lie,' I declared.

'Sorry, what? Potential what?' Adam asked.

---

* https://vm.tiktok.com/ZMFqmTcVB/

'P' IS FOR 'PARENTS' ...

My relationship with my four-year-old daughter is very similar to the one I have with my mother and indeed similar to hers with her mother. The main theme here is that all of us laugh with each other and, most importantly, laugh at ourselves. Humour is ageless. It's a tonic, it conquers all and unites people. In my teenage years I remember being in fits of laughter with my nanny (not paid help, my actual nan) and my four-year-old is often in hysterics with her nana. But not at silly kid stuff – proper p*ss-takes out of each other, sarcastic jokes, pretending to be serious but cracking up at the end after a glint in the eye. And that type of relationship between any ages is fruitful and timeless.

I'll give you an example of the type of LOLs Cressy and I have together. Now, a walk isn't something the kids would necessarily CHOOSE to do as their preferred activity, but once they're out in the fresh air, dodging manure and tripping over potholes, they rather like it. The loop we usually do through the fields at the back of our house, down the lane and back home is exactly a mile long and takes us an hour and a half. So that's nice. This isn't because they have unusually short legs for their age, or that it's too far for them, it's because of the distractions along the way. For the most part, I welcome them. What parent wouldn't want their kids to spend time out in the countryside, breathing the fresh country air? But sometimes it's not so great. It can mean taking 13 minutes trying to figure out where a tree stump root is going, or trying to persuade them that climbing on a makeshift swing suspended above a puddle of sloppy mud will end in tears. What I really love though are the chats. Like the one I had with Cressy not so long ago. It was late in the day and very cold. She was enjoying the walk and we were wrapped in puffer jackets and wellies, squelching through the mud. I could see the mist from her mouth as she was breathing in and out, and it all felt good. Cressy turned to me after a couple of minutes' silence.

Cressy: 'This is the life, darlin'.'

Me: 'Yes, it is. Sorry, did you say ...?'

Cressy: 'I said, "This is the life, darlin'."'

And with that, she went into cockney character even more and pointed her finger at me as she said it.

Me, cracking up: 'Yes, I thought that's what you said. I'm not going to lie, I don't know where to start with so much of that sentence. But let's start with the accent and also where you've heard that.'

Cressy: 'Well, you often say "This is the life" and I added in "darlin'."'

Me: 'Yeah, I got the first bit. I was asking more about the bit you added in.'

Cressy: 'It's an accent. I'm doing a different accent, Mummy. JEEZ!'

Me: 'Yes, I know THAT. It's more a questi–'

Cressy interrupted: 'Do you want me to teach you how to say it?'

Me: 'Yeah, sod it! Why not?'

And for the next eight minutes, my four-year-old taught me a line I'm pretty sure I was able to say in the first place even with the accent, but doubting myself more and more as she condemned my pronunciation every time. The more she said it, the more aggressive her finger pointing got and the harsher-sounding her acute cockney accent was, which seemed rather inspiring but slightly odd, given the warmth and friendliness of the words she was actually saying. If I closed my eyes, I could have been listening to Bill Sikes from *Oliver!* I didn't know whether to be thoroughly impressed or utterly petrified.

*   *   *

Anyway, one January night around 10 p.m. I got a phone call from my mother's neighbour. I didn't recognise the number but picked up. She said that my mother had fallen on her patio in her garden, but that she was with her. I wondered how this could have happened. My father passed away in 1994 when I was in my early teens (more on which later), and even though my mother lives alone she is a fairly active 67-year-old. By that, I mean she takes her dog for a walk twice a day. But seriously, she's not some 92-year-old who would easily fall and need a hip replacement anytime soon. It was quickly brought to my attention that she had accidentally locked herself out while letting the dog out for her evening wee and realised the keys were in her bedroom, which could be accessed by an exterior set of (rotten) wooden steps from the garden, leading up to a sort of balcony, which had double doors to her bedroom, which she knew were unlocked. As she didn't have her phone, and wasn't sure what else to do, she thought she would spread her weight across each step and attempt the journey up there.

It must be said that any garden party or BBQ we have had at my mother's has always included the words 'kids don't go on those stairs, they're not safe'. The two stone in weight child must not put a foot on those stairs, but a 12-stone adult, when faced with having to knock on a neighbour's door in her nightie at 10 p.m., can obviously give it a go. I learnt that she had got all the way up the 11 stairs, reached the top and then the whole thing had given way. She ended up crashing down 10 feet to the concrete and was in excruciating pain. It was −2 outside and the shock of pain and bitterly cold weather meant she wasn't quite with it. As she recounted to me when I asked what she did next, she laughed and said, 'Well, being outside in the garden of a detached house at 10 p.m., I didn't hold out much hope of anyone coming to any rescue, so I feebly said, "Heeeeelp" not very loudly, but a few times, and to my surprise my neighbours came and said their dog alerted them. It wasn't my finest hour, Ra.'

I don't care what their dog is called, I have named it Lassie.

Long story short, she refused an ambulance and went to bed, with her neighbour's help getting into the house. The next day she realised, maybe she did need some help. And she did. She had fractured her pelvis in two places (we found out later) and with the help of two paramedics, the fire department, eight firemen, an ambulance and some morphine she was on her way to the hospital. Tough cookie, but Jesus there are easier ways to get attention.

*   *   *

Around the same time, *YOU Magazine* wrote to me in my DMs saying they were doing a big feature on comedians who had risen to fame on TikTok during the pandemic and that they would like to do an interview and photo shoot with me. My first thought was, maybe they'd like to actually talk to a comedian who had risen to fame during the pandemic, but hey, who was I to argue?

Was this the first bit of great exposure that could catapult me into Hollywood next week? Probably not, but it was a teensy-weensy step.

It suddenly occurred to me that I might want to lose the stone in weight I'd put on in the last year before this shoot. Do-able in two weeks, right? Hang on, don't try to do that. That's ridiculous. I'm joking. Maybe just 13 pounds. No. Joking. Sh*t. Basically, DON'T try to lose a stone in two weeks. Done. No lawyers banging on my door today.

But I do want to lose a bit of weight, so sue me. I'm heavier than – and not as healthy as – I want to be. A while ago I did a TikTok on healthy snacking while eating a whole bag of radishes in the car. OK, I do genuinely love radishes and I also know it's important to promote healthy eating where possible. You know, use your platform and all that. So, as an 'influencer', I let the audience know that I was able to go from 12 stone 3lb to 12 stone 1lb in less than two and a half months, just by snacking healthily between meals.

What those main meals consisted of was neither here nor there. Needless to say, I put any thoughts of losing any weight at all to the back of my mind and focused on scheduling the interview.

*   *   *

I know I've had you on tenterhooks wondering what happened to my mum after her fall. Well, after eight weeks, one IKEA bed delivered for her living room, a minifridge I set up next to said bed containing mini-cans of G&T which she never asked for, some gentle exercises and a commode by the bed, she was on the mend. It wasn't the most dignified of times, she said, particularly when she's normally so independent, but I suppose it could have been worse. At least she, quite literally, had a pot to p*ss in.

'I' IS FOR 'INDOORS' ...

Some parents jump for joy at the prospect of school holidays, while others can't wait to send their little treasures straight back to the classroom. What we can all probably agree on, though – hopefully? Maybe? – is that spending quality time together on family days out is as good as it gets. Here, the key word is 'out'. The good times, the best times – (and this is some kind of parenting law) – are most definitely *not* to be had in the house.

Who are these lunatics pretending arts and crafts and baking at home are fun? No sooner am I sitting down with my actually very patient and adorable daughter to do one of my – I mean, *her* – favourite princess puzzles than her little brother comes up and destroys all of the pieces we have put together by swiping them in a windscreen wiper motion across the table and onto the floor. And if I play monster trucks with him, five minutes in I'll inevitably hear my darling daughter say something along the lines of, 'Mummy, could we put the stencils on my piggy bank now, but without Monty because he'll ruin it?' And if I leave them on their own to play, I get four minutes, followed by a scream of, 'Mummy, Monty won't give my Barbie back and now she only has one leg!' Followed by tears, mayhem, Monty throwing the Barbie back to her and then hiding in their toy box. I'm not sure what the hiding's about – it's like he thinks I'm going to come upstairs with a wooden spoon to whack him on the bum, like it's 1976.

Tangent: I actually never got hit anywhere and certainly not with a wooden spoon, but I have heard LOADS of people, friends of mine, talk about this wooden spoon. Why wasn't a hand good enough? I've no bloody clue. It's a bit barbaric if you ask me. Is it because they'd rather use a hard utensil than hurt their hand while hitting their own child?

Things have come on a bit since then, thank God, although I was shocked to learn from the Citizens Advice website that hitting a child isn't illegal if it is deemed a 'reasonable punishment'. Crikey. How do you even measure that? Personally, I've never been on board with the idea of hitting a child. I'd never want to hit or physically hurt an adult, so I certainly don't want to inflict pain on my children. Sorry, I lie. I don't want to physically hurt an adult, except if they're harming an animal or a child. Then I genuinely want to kick the sh*t out of them. I know, I wouldn't be able to in real life, but I can talk a good talk. Besides, I sounded bloody hard for about three seconds then.

I've been called a snowflake before for having this stance on smacking children. By friends I know and random people on social media. Their usual response is, 'Well, I was smacked and I turned out OK.' 'Did you though?' I joke. 'But could you have turned out better?'

I'm not saying that I don't get hugely frustrated or that I haven't lost my sh*t occasionally. Of course I do and of course I have. Sometimes – when things feel out of control or you're nagging your darlings for the thirteenth time to please get dressed, or after four times of telling one not to hit the other – they test you with one step further and a hair pull after a night of very little sleep, which is when I get to the end of my tether. I lose it for a second in the raising voice stakes. Sometimes I grab one to take them off the other quickly before they get hurt and other times when they are both safe and just not listening to my pleas, I take myself off outside, away from the situation when I feel it escalating. It's actually incredible what a few deep breaths in the fresh air and a shot of tequila can do to calm you down and get a better response from your kids. I'm kidding! You need way more than a shot.

I've been there but I genuinely don't believe any sort of hitting or force is the answer. My number-one reason for this, and maybe selfishly, is I don't ever want my children to be scared of me or to cower after they've done something naughty in anticipation of what will happen. That would break my heart. Which is why I was astonished to learn from Entertainmentdaily.co.uk that we in the UK are one of only four countries in Europe where it is still legal for you to hit your children if it is for 'reasonable punishment'. We need to change, so we can start to protect our children and support parents to use positive and effective alternatives to physical punishment. If that makes me a snowflake, please make me a blizzard.

Back to the holidays ... Oh yes, trying to stay at home during school holidays can be a nightmare. When I first had kids, I remember thinking the baby stage was boring. Are babies cute? Yes. Mainly because of their size, or their first smile or giggle. That's it. Do they do anything but sleep, cry, eat and crap? No. I was one of the few who almost wished away the baby phase. I couldn't wait for the day we would communicate beyond me just talking at them in what I thought was a cute voice (but to others is cringeworthy) and them staring gormlessly back at me. I had images of us baking cakes and laughing while getting flour in our hair, finger painting and giggling as we playfully put paint on each other's noses ... you get the idea. Imagine my surprise when this day eventually came and turned out to be nothing like this fairy-tale description.

Although I love cooking, I have never 'baked' anything in my life. But that was surely part of the fun, right? Wrong. At the time, my kids were almost three and one and a half, which I now know is WAY too young for this type of activity. It started badly: Monty wanted to do exactly what his big sister was doing: cracking eggs. I thought I would let him – after all, they only learn by trying. Then, I turned to have a quick glance at the recipe and grab the butter from the fridge. I hadn't noticed that Monty's eggy handiwork had turned the floor into a slip'n'slide of egg whites for my legs to enjoy and in my panic reached for the nearest thing, which happened to be Cressy's arm. I landed heavily on my coccyx, pulled Cressy down with me and we ended up in a tangle of limbs on the floor. Monty sat giggling, eating melted chocolate from the bowl and surveying the damage that his nine broken eggs had created.

'Who wants to go to the adventure park?' I cried.

Going out is a different ball game altogether. One of our favourite places to go 'out' with the kids is the pub. Wait, hear me out. I genuinely love the role the humble pub plays in our British culture.

Our tradition and heritage revolves around many things that we also have in common with other countries that have long histories: ancient buildings, old cobbled streets, crap beaches. But one thing which I have never found in another country other than Great Britain is a 'proper' pub. You know, the kind you see in Richard Curtis movies.

In his 17th century diary, Samuel Pepys described the pub as the 'Heart of England'. There are all sorts of pubs of course, and while no two pubs are ever the same, British ones do share many quintessential characteristics: low ceilings, wooden beams, open log fireplaces and a regular called Dave. I bloody love them. And so, it seems, do my children.

To be fair, this is probably down to Adam and me, unless my two under-fives crept out of the house after bedtime to play Barbie and dinosaurs in The Rose and Crown. In fact, three weeks after Cressy was born, I met my mum, uncle and grandmother for lunch in The Two Sawyers pub and that was her first experience of these perfect, informal places. Although I love a posh restaurant every now and again (see 'W' for 'Wanky Restaurants'), I much prefer a casual, easy-going environment, where muddy wellies are welcome if you bang them at the door, black labs lie by their owners' feet in front of a roaring fire and the giggles of children dissipate as they run down the beer garden towards the pub climbing frame, while grown-ups clink glasses of Pimms. Often, Sunday lunch takes the form of a meet-up with family in a pub garden, Saturday is a pint of ale in a country pub at the end of a long walk, and Christmas means sipping mulled wine while excitedly queueing to see Father Christmas in a makeshift grotto in the 'snug bar' of a pub, before remembering you left your kids and husband at home. So many of my great memories with friends and family have taken place in pubs.

Now, my kids have become lovers of them too. At school pick up, Cressy asks, 'Can we go to the pub with Bella and Laurie?' In practise, pubs are great for kids: we can choose one with an outside area and a mini play-ground where they can burn off steam while the grown-ups have a post work, pre-bedtime catch up over a drink and a snack. But the fact that going to the pub with the kids after school is legitimately a great thing to do doesn't make it any less embarrassing when they beg, 'Please can we go to The Queens Inn,' in front of their teachers.

The first time this happened, my response went something like this:

Nervous laughter

'Cressy, you silly billy! Well done for remembering such a complicated name but I don't even know if there IS a pub called that around here. It's funny that you even said that because it's not usually something we do. You normally like going home.'

'No I don't, and I remember that name because we've been there loads of times. It's just up the road from here, remember?'

'Oh, yes, that Queen's Inn.'

'Yes, you like the padron peppers and we like the honey sausages.'

'No, Laurie likes the padron peppers. I like the squid. Wait, what?'

And that is how our kids became obsessed with pubs. And I am completely fine with that. But we do also go further afield.

One of our favourite trips is going to Hastings for a stroll, enjoying the playground, spending half an hour in the arcades putting two-pence pieces in the slots to win a tiny pot of slime, and eating fish and chips sitting on the beach. And sometimes the kids even join in.

On one of these trips, I spent £26 on three seafront

rides for the kids in the first half an hour. Naturally, I wondered whether there might be any other over-priced attractions nearby and, to my delight, I spotted two more. But even though I was desperate to burn a hole in my wallet by going on an oversized big wheel (which I wasn't sure my very young kids would love or hate, anyway), I decided that a £12.50 fish and chips each would have a larger enjoyment success rate (even though I'd still need to remortgage my house). We decided to go all rustic and sit on the beach to eat them. 'Sod it,' I thought, 'let's go wild and have them open, not wrapped.' Cressy stepped out of the shop first and at that moment a colossal seagull (who, if I'm honest, could have done with a stint at Slimming World) swooped down and pecked at Cressy's battered sausage. Cressy held it tighter, which only wound it up more as the bird flapped over the top of her head. Despite her valiant attempt, she let out a long scream, threw the sausage up in the air and ran zig-zagging down the street. I felt bad for laughing uncontrollably, until three more gulls started diving for my chips. 'Just don't get my fish!' I shouted, waving my arms about. I'm not sure what I thought negotiating with a seagull would achieve, but they weren't playing ball. Having succumbed to giving these monsters about £14 worth of food, we headed to the beach to finish what we had left.

The day was drawing to a close when Cressy spotted a cable car on the hillside. 'Mummy, we must do that! Look, it's a small train on a hill.'

'That's closed today, unfortunately, Cress.'

'Why is it moving up the hill?'

'They're testing it. Maintenance. It's Sunday. It's definitely closed. So sorry. But we can absolutely spend a fortune on it next time.'

LIFE LESSON
ACCORDING TO CLARA BATTEN: 2

**ALWAYS TEACH YOUR CHILDREN
TO TELL THE TRUTH.**

Also, lying to your kids to protect your bank account is fine. But even when a day out turns into a slight nightmare, it's still infinitely better than the nightmare of staying indoors with them all day.

'N' IS FOR 'NEW YEAR'S RESOLUTIONS' …

Every January, like most people, my husband and I discuss New Year's resolutions.

In the January mid-pandemic, I said to Adam, 'Don't even try to get me to do the whole no-booze, dry January, or cutting out carbs, eating healthier thing. Not during a lockdown with two little people in a pandemic.' I got in there before he had a chance to even take a breath to talk.

He said, 'Well, no – I was thinking more like exercise. Getting a bit fitter. You're always saying the daily walks are great but aren't quite cutting it for you, what with the kids getting tired easily, but that you think the fresh air and exercise really help with your state of mind. You keep saying you just feel like running to the end of that field and that you would love a break now and then and that pumping some air around your body would really …'

'Yes, OK! What I SAY and what I MEAN aren't always the same thing, but I get what you're saying.'

'I didn't say it – you did.'

'OK. Look, let's not split hairs. If you would like to run, I would be more than happy to join you and support you in getting fitter.'

'Hang on, what?'

Anyway, long story short: we decided to run. I was excited by this prospect. Mainly for the reasons Adam had pointed out. Mental health, catching a 30-minute break and getting fitter. But we needed an incentive to make sure we did it, and often.

Adam suggested we do it for charity.

'Yes, like train for a 5k run by getting out there a few days a week. There's this thing called Couch to 5k. We could end up doing a 5k in, like, July?'

'OR … run every day for 100 days. Starting tomorrow. And we can't take one day off. And if you do, you've failed. Or you have to start again. Oh, and it has to be a mile at least, each day.'

'Sorry, what?' Talk about going from the sublime to the ridiculous. Who needs to ease themselves into these things anyway?

'OK, yes. YES. Let's do it. Can I choose the charity, or at least put one forward?' I asked.

I had read in an article by Childline that child abuse had risen by 1,500 per cent year on year in March 2020. It scared me enormously to think that so many children had been put through so much for a whole year. The statistics were horrifying. The NSPCC and their mantra to combat child abuse seemed the most fitting and it didn't take

Adam any convincing to agree. It must be said, we didn't run together, at the same time. I mean, our kids are pretty independent but even I draw the line at leaving them alone in the house.

We got 11 days of running out of the way and, surprisingly, it was going pretty well. I was vlogging every day to try and keep the generous donations coming, although I can't say they were the most riveting videos: 'Day 1 of 100 days of running for the NSPCC'. 'Day 5 of 100 days of Running for the NSPCC', some jogging and then some pretty pathetic pants of exhaustion. Already close to raising the £2,000 target we had set 11 days in, then Monty tested positive for Covid at the end of January.

We had to isolate for 10 days, which meant we would have to run around our garden a mile every day to keep this up. I got into my running gear and in the pouring rain, I stepped onto the very waterlogged garden after two days of downpour. Having an actual river running through our garden means it often looks like a lake after torrential or relentless rain and it had looked like this the day before. I couldn't contain my excitement at the prospect of running on this new terrain for the next 10 days. What fun it would be. Needless to say, within 15 seconds of 'running' on this marsh, I had twisted my ankle and fallen straight into the muddy swamp. I jumped up, remembering Adam and the kids were waiting for me in the car. Like a drowned rat, I limped towards them with mud splattered across my face and body.

I looked at the kids with a smirk on my face, raising my eyebrows, pointing towards my face in slow motion, as if I was some sort of children's entertainer. Adam looked confused.

'You should see the state of the other guy,' I said.

It wasn't my finest hour. I didn't try it again.

We decided to terminate the run and start over when we could run on a normal pavement again. Some might say it's actually nicer to run on some sort of grass terrain – and very possibly better for you too – but no, it is in fact very relaxing running on a busy A-road pavement, inhaling carbon monoxide fumes with every breath, the sound of cars whizzing past your ears. Either way, anything was going to be better than the swamp.

LIFE LESSON
ACCORDING TO CLARA BATTEN: 3

DON'T EXERCISE IF YOU THINK YOU MIGHT BE ALLERGIC TO IT, LIKE ME.

I did it once and my skin flushed, my heart raced,
I sweated and got very short of breath.
Bloody dangerous.

My other New Year's Resolution was to make less of a tw*t of myself at the kids' school. Recently, I dropped them off there. That's not me making some profound statement, waiting for a 'Mother of the Year' award. It's me about to tell you a little tale about an embarrassing moment I had not so long ago. I had finished dropping Cressy off at her classroom and was rushing back to my car to get home for a call I had 20 minutes later. I was avoiding eye contact with any parents in case I ended up having a 35-minute chat in the car park with another mum or dad craving some 'adult time'. Thankful that nobody had intercepted me, I jumped in the driver's seat. Closing my eyes, I put my head back and breathed a sigh of relief as if I had just completed an MI5 mission. I pulled my keys out of my pocket and opened my eyes to the most pristine, cleaner-than-clean car I had ever seen. Either a valet service had very generously and maybe a bit inappropriately got to work on my sh*t-hole of a car in the eight minutes it had taken me to drop Cressy off, or I was, um, in the wrong one. Knowing that no valet service in the history of valeting had ever set up shop in a school car park, my main objective was to get out of that car and get to mine as quickly as possible without drawing attention to myself, or the owner of the vehicle I was in the driving seat of spotting me. This was ambitious: I couldn't remember where I had parked my car in the first place. I got out of the car, as if it was mine (whatever that looks like) and walked nonchalantly towards where I thought my actual car might be parked. As I did so, my friend Polly shouted from the opposite direction: 'Clara, what the bloody hell were you doing in that car, you daft cow?'

'SSHH,' I said, 'just checking it out. Turns out, it's a very nice car. We might get one.' I had realised the car I got into wasn't even the same make, model or even colour as mine. The only similarity was that it was an SUV. I strode towards my car, hoping the owner hadn't witnessed my antics during the last five minutes and gesticulated with my head for Polly to join me at my car.

'F*cking hell, thank God only you saw! That could have been really embarrassing.' I got in my car and added, 'Don't tell anyone I did that, will you?'

'What, like that lot over there?' and with that she nodded towards a separate class building where two teachers and three parents were laughing their heads off.

'Yeah, like that lot.'

FFS.

'M' IS FOR 'MCDONALD'S' ...

I'm a savoury foods fan. I'd much prefer to eat last night's salad with a teensy-weensy bit (OK, a bowl) of pasta for breakfast, instead of a bowl of Weetabix or porridge, which I've worked out would actually be half the calories. But I'M HAVING SALAD. I still can't figure that one out.

Anyway, talking of McDonald's, we are helping my mother move out of her house at the moment. She is up and about slowly following her accident, giving us very clear instructions on what needs to be done and where things need to go. Completion is in a week. There's a lot to do. (The McDonald's part will make sense soon, I promise.) We have arranged one of those removal companies who actually pack everything for you and then move it. Genius. But in all honesty, the packing is only a little bit helpful, as we have to sort through everything my grandmother owned first (they shared a house together until she passed away a few years ago). Now, I don't mean to tar all old people with the same brush, but bloody hell, do they hoard – and I mean all of them.

Luckily, my mother likes to get rid of stuff. Or, *unluck-ily* for us, as it means we also have to sift through it all and put into categories of 'keep', 'auction' (#middleclassgrand-parents), 'charity' and 'skip'. No, all jokes aside, it's extremely therapeutic to get rid of stuff and have a good old clear out. Mummy (yes, I'm 39 and I still call her 'Mummy') is so excited about getting out of a large, hard-to-manage house and into a smaller cottage after three years of it being on the market that we are all happy to be there with bells on. At least so long as fast food is a regular lunch option.

We are heading over to her house again but need to pick up some supplies en route from the big Sainsbury's in Hastings. Now, I have a love/hate relationship with this place. It's the largest supermarket within 20 minutes of us (love), also selling what I would call a spectacular choice of clothing attire (love and hate). Unfortunately, they put this right in front of my face as I walk in. Needless to say, I end up spending £40 more on my Sainsbury's trip due to the purchasing of children's clothing, which I may or may not have needed, and, inevitably, a standard £16 (reduced from £20) jumper which, in fact, I promise I DO need.

Anyway, the love/hate thing isn't ACTUALLY to do with the shop itself, it's to do with the big golden arches of McDonald's on the bus stops leading up to it, pointing to where I'm about to go (Sainsbury's) but letting me know it's right there next to it. Obviously, being the caring mother I am, and not wanting my children to starve, having only eaten Haribo in the last two hours, who am I not to make the three-minute detour to the drive-thru and give them the 'fish burger' they always want from 'Old McDonald'? Looks like everyone has the same idea. The queue is ridiculous. My four-year-old very maturely says, 'Mummy, there's a massive queue so maybe we should just go to the orange shop and get to Nana's as she needs our help.'

'NO! ARE YOU KIDDING ME? You need lunch. JESUS, Nana needs lunch! It would be really selfish and quite irresponsible of me to abandon this mission now.'

Really, I had just seen an advert on their board in the queue saying, 'The Grand Big Mac is back'. Well, that was it. I was destined to spend the next 27 minutes in a drive-thru queue, while on a diet, late to see my mother (who has just had an accident and is moving house), just to get my hands on a Grand Big Mac. I've officially sunk lower than my attempt to run a mile on my quagmire garden.

I bought two x Filet-O-Fish meals, three x Grand Big Mac meals, two x chocolate milkshakes and two boxes of 20 chicken nuggets – just in case. I don't know what it's 'in case' of, but I would feel a bit uneasy leaving a McDonald's with just a standard meal for each person. What if I need something else? If you're not spending at least a third of your initial order on extras, you might as well starve to death. And when I say 'extras', I mean chicken nuggets and also mozzarella dippers, chicken selects and occasionally those 'limited time' chilli cheese bites which are like molten lava if you eat them immediately, but worth every mouth blister for the sensational fusion of green chilli and melted mozzarella. But everyone buys chicken nuggets as an extra. They're easy to share, great as an immediate chaser to a burger and amazing half an hour later, if you just need something to pick at after scoffing a Grand Big Mac, large fries and a chocolate milkshake. Well, I *am* watching what I eat. And by that, I mean I'm hoping to be able to scoff in the car while watching myself doing it in my rear-view mirror.

Cressy stopped me from doing this, and eating in the car full stop, by reminding me of our objective. But she didn't use that word. She just said something like, 'No, Mummy, stop thinking about eating for once and just get to Nana's.'

We got to my mother's house and though ecstatic about the prospect of going through more VHS tapes, wondering how we might get them onto DVD even though none of us owned a DVD player anymore, I just wanted to sink my teeth into a Grand Big Mac. My willpower being tested this immensely on the journey from Maccy D's to my mum's is the absolute definition of restraint. Seventeen minutes of smelling but not digging in is something I wouldn't want my worst enemy to go through – and I'm not even being dramatic.

When I got the go-ahead from Cressy, I opened the bags with anticipation, to discover they were full of fries and fish things and chicken stuff, but NO Grand Big Macs.

NO. GRAND. BIG. MACS?

Fuming is an understatement.

I don't want to talk about it anymore, I'm still a little bit scarred. Sorry, maybe just one more thing, I didn't even pull them up on it as I couldn't be arsed to drive back and so, essentially, I ended up eating eight chicken nuggets and some fries, which is basically a starter.

Bottom line: let's forget this. Really, forget it, guys. It's FINE.

*   *   *

As we were packing, Mummy unearthed a photo of my father when he was Monty's age, two and a half. When he died when I was 13, my elder brothers Ben and Theo stepped into a fatherly role, particularly Ben. Although it was so long ago and I was relatively young, I was a real daddy's girl so those 13 years for me were formative and important, and still are. I remember so much. The smell of his Eau Sauvage aftershave, Extra Strong mints and slight cigar smell on his cold suit after I waited up, sitting on the stairs for him to come home from work (he was a big workaholic). I had an affinity with him, like I knew we would always get on, be OK, however much of my little (OK, BIG) strops he 'occasionally' had to put up with. I loved him dearly and in my eyes he could do no wrong. I guess that's what happens when you see very little of one of the most important people to you.

My mother was always there. The rock. Putting up with anything that was thrown at her. Three kids, almost single-handedly raising them on her own, leaving Daddy's home-cooked meal in the microwave ready for his return when we were all in bed. Being an adult now, it's crazy to look back and think that this was normal. I have said to my mother, since growing up and having my own children, that I don't think I could stay with someone who worked so much. Mainly because Adam helps with bedtime and is bloody good at DIY. Mum agreed that she found it hard, but she did it for us. Besides, it was the only 'testing' part of an otherwise wonderful marriage.

Saying that, I also understand why my father was doing it. He was tremendously ambitious but came from a very 'normal' background and wanted more for us than what he had, I suppose. He wasn't an arsehole is what I'm trying to say. He was doing it for us and I understood that back then. Like I said, I thought it was normal until I stayed at friends' houses and saw their fathers come back from the office at 7 p.m. and have supper with us. I suppose, in retrospect, I just really appreciate what my mother has always done for us and I'm so sorry that the stress of what Daddy was trying to do for us ended in his departure way too soon. He was a magnificent father when he was there – I just wish it had been more.

So, the photo. When I looked at it and sent it to family members, and four of my closest friends, they all thought it either looked identical to Monty or WAS Monty in a sepia-filtered photo. But it was my dad. And Monty looks identical to Adam. Sh*t! Which means Adam looks like my father, which also means either I have some minor issues going on, or I've married my dad's illegitimate son. Brilliant.

*   *   *

As we approached Valentine's Day, my biggest question to my husband was, would he like to be at the dining table for supper or should we sit on the sofa with it on our laps, watching *Below Deck*? It didn't take long for us both to opt for the latter.

Some will know this little treat of a programme, although many won't admit it. I have no shame, so I'll tell you about it. *Below Deck* is a reality TV show about a charter season on a superyacht and the 'struggles' they go through as a crew; aka tantrums, fights, slagging off the guests, getting drunk on their days off, narcissistic chefs and overpaid patrons. You're welcome. And you can look forward to me waxing lyrical about my other reality TV passions later in this very book, you lucky things!

Look, on Valentine's night, we can't go out at 7 p.m. for a meal and drinks, kid-free, so we would both prefer, after a long day of working from home, to sit with a glass of wine or a gin and tonic, supper on our laps, watching some mindless TV. I chose fillet steak to cook as this is one of his favourites. Nothing to do with any bribe and absolutely nothing to do with the fact it would take a maximum of eight minutes to cook and that would mean a potential binge of three hour-long episodes by the time we felt we needed to go to bed. I made creamed spinach with the steak. And fries. And sautéed garlic mushrooms. OK, got carried away. I didn't do mushrooms – I should have done though.

The second very important question to Adam around Valentine's Day was, is it OK if we don't buy each other presents? I'm not a high maintenance girl – OK, lady. Sod that, woman. Why am I finding it so difficult to label myself? But Adam is very decent and would always want to get me SOMETHING. This time though, we needed an understanding between us that neither was allowed to get the other presents and for a very good reason. Adam lost his business pretty much overnight at the start of the pandemic (I'll stop talking about the 'p' word very soon, I promise, but it's important to give you some background). He had a software company with his business partner Charlie, which serviced the hospitality and events indus-try. Obviously, that went to sh*t overnight when everything closed and we couldn't leave our homes, so things for us changed quite quickly. All of a sudden there was little to no income so my bright idea to start making funny videos online, which could take quite a bit of time in some cases, not make any money, gain me roughly a mere 1,000 followers in the first six weeks but may just get me an acting job down the line (which isn't a competitive industry at all) was a winner. JESUS, just call me Steve Jobs! That said, I'm sure he could have stretched to a Grand Big Mac.

QUOTES BY CRESSY

After drying her hands.

Me: 'Why are they still wet? They feel wet. Why don't you dry them a bit before bed?'

Cressy: 'They're not WET. They're cold. I washed them with cold water. That's why they feel cold,' and with a glint in her eye, she says, 'Do you even know what you're talking about? Sometimes I wonder.'

LIFE LESSON
ACCORDING TO CLARA BATTEN: 4

I BELIEVE THAT ONE OF THE MAIN REASONS WE ARE HERE IS TO ENJOY EACH OTHER'S COOKING AND APPRECIATE FOOD.

If the food happens to be a burger and the other person cooking is a bloke with a McDonald's cap on, so be it.

'D' IS FOR 'DRESSING UP' ...

(The kids, not me, you weirdos)

Every year, I feel like as soon as we're back to school after the Christmas break, it's time to break up for the Easter holidays. And every Easter, I have the same thought, 'The kids will be asked to bring something into school, or do something Easter-related. Well, that's exciting. For them. And terrifying for me.' The fact of the matter is, I rarely read school emails unless they say 'Important' or 'Critical' or 'Danger'. No school emails ever say 'Danger', but if they DID title the subject matter 'Danger' while telling me there's ice across the road at the bottom of the lane and advising I might want to take another route, I would probably actually read it, therefore know about this advice and most likely take it.

I have two kids at two different schools until Monty can join Cressy's in a few months, thus twice the amount of emails and considering half of the emails are sent en masse to all parents when they're only relevant to about five per cent of us, I feel I'm somewhat warranted in my lack of desire to want to click on any of these emails just in case they are relevant to me. On that note, I think it should be someone's job to literally read all the school emails and condense them down into the bare minimum of what an individual actually needs to know, preferably in bullet points. It would be a full-time job.

Sometimes I don't even keep up with the school WhatsApp group, which is definitely more interesting than the school emails as it includes messages about items of clothing which have mistakenly been taken home by a different child. Sometimes in my boredom I like to play a guessing game with myself as to who will be the one who ended up with it.

Yes, the long evenings fly by in my house.

But seriously, there are some top girls (yeah, I just called us 'girls') in this group. Some good friends, some acquaintances and some I haven't even met properly. There's banter, a lot of support, some passing on of second-hand uniforms and occasionally a little bit of drama, which is great fun if you have a spare 10 minutes and some popcorn.

Occasionally, this WhatsApp group contains the word 'wine' – not often, but when it does, it always piques my interest so it's worth checking in just in case. Sometimes I even type the word 'wine' into the search at the top of the group in case I missed it among the other 400 messages. A friend pointed out, though, that it could just say, 'Let's go for drinks' so now I search 'drinks', 'gin' and 'cocktails' as well. It's also brilliant for checking anything I may have missed in the school emails which may be pertinent to me and for that, I will always be grateful. Easter is always one of those cases.

In fairness to me, I DID check into Cressy's school WhatsApp group, albeit probably two days too late, given the subject matter that they were talking about. I had 56 unread messages and, boy, I wished I had joined when there had been three. I won't say too much here, but the words 'Easter' and 'bonnet' were mentioned more than I could care for.

What even is an Easter bonnet? I don't wish to be dramatic, but my heart was pounding a little at the first few messages I read. There was a lot of 'homemade' chat, a lot of 'Rupert really got stuck into creating his today' and 'Ooh, it's actually been a lot of fun making this with Evie'. The icing on the cake for me was reading 'we are currently sticking on fluffy bunnies and carrots but Hugo isn't letting me get a look-in'. Erm, sorry, creating WHAT exactly? I scrolled quicker than I have ever scrolled to find out exactly what we were meant to be doing.

When Cressy was two, Grandma handmade her a sweet little chicken as an Easter hat for nursery so not only did I think that was in fact an Easter bonnet, I now had to figure out why the others were using such different terminology regarding theirs, which sounded nothing like what we'd had in the past. Never mind, it was cute and beautiful and tonight it was destined to be her hat for a third year running.

Luckily, we always put it in the same place: in a little drawer at the bottom of her bookshelf. I went straight there to get it. It was 8 p.m. the night before this Easter extravaganza was happening at her school. It wasn't there. I didn't want to panic Cressy but she had heard me talking about it: 'Oh yes, I love that Easter hat. Oh, Mummy, are we wearing those to school tomorrow?'

Oh, sh*t.

'Exactly, darling, it's a HAT. You're right. But yes, you can. Well, maybe. If we can find it. I'm sure we will but if not, you will have something very special to take.' I'm not sure I should have included 'very special' in that sentence. After searching her room, I put her to bed, reassured her and furiously searched our room and any other place we thought it could possibly be. A full hour of two grown adults looking in every toy box, kids' tent and cupboard full of crap.

It was nowhere.

Hang on, I could order on Amazon Prime and get it delivered to school the next day. But what delivery instructions would I need to put on there in order to get it to the correct building and, if they were outside playing or at lunch, which 'safe place' could the driver leave it at?

Oh God, I've officially sunk to the lowest depths of parenthood.

That was not an option so I started googling 'Easter bonnets near me'. I mean, seriously? I still wasn't sure exactly what an Easter bonnet was (or how one was going to be 'near me'). Really, no idea. But the fact other mums had talked about sticking fluffy bunnies and all sorts on them wasn't filling me with the greatest hope that whatever I managed to achieve in the next 12 hours, at night, with most of it incorporating sleep, would be anything close to what sounded like these masterpieces.

The next morning Cressy asked if I had managed to find the bonnet. I said I hadn't but that I would sort it, I wouldn't let her down. Being the sweet, mature four-year-old that she is (and she really is, bless her), she said, 'It's alright, Mummy, I know you tried.' And with tears in my eyes, that was that: whatever it took I was getting an Easter bloody bonnet to her that morning, no matter what. Once I had figured out what it was.

After dropping off Monty and taking Cressy to school, kissing her goodbye and giving her a comforting nod I'd be back, I got a message from a friend saying, 'By the way, mate, Sainsbury's are doing Easter bonnets for £2. Result.'

Destination: Sainsbury's. I just had to muster up the willpower to avoid the detour to get a double sausage Egg McMuffin next door. I quickly found a Sainsbury's worker to point me in the right direction: Easter bonnet £2. Easter bonnet kit £4. Done deal. The £4 one it was. Mother of the Year right there. But I still felt inadequate. Hang on, what were those little beauties I could see? Only Galaxy Enchanted mini eggs (this is not an ad). I bought three packets for Cressy and her friends to enjoy (massive points), some rainbow mini-fluffy chicks and some normal yellow ones in case they got freaked out by the non-realistic ones. Done. At almost 10 a.m. I was heading back to her school, both ashamed and elated by the morning's proceedings.

I got back to her school, so excited, ringing the doorbell with a bag full of goodies. One of the teachers answered.

'Hi, is Cressy there? I've got some little things for her, one being an Easter bonnet she can decorate herself with her friends.' Almost more smug than how I'd feel had she done it without her friends, as so many of them had.

'Oh, I'm so sorry! They've gone out into the forest to search for Easter eggs with the Easter Bunny … with their Easter bonnets on.'

'But Cressy didn't have one?'

'No, but we bought these kits just in case any parents forgot. She's made one. Don't worry, she has one.'

Slowly and quietly, 'Were these kits £4 from Sainsbury's?' I'm not sure why this was important to me at the time and why I was saying it so creepily.

'Not sure.'

She *was* sure though, she was sure that she was looking at a mum who was having some sort of breakdown.

I welled up; I actually couldn't stand it. I wanted to run through that forest until I found my daughter, to give her a hug and tell her Mummy had brought one to her and extra things too. But I wasn't allowed. I wasn't allowed to run like a lunatic, in the middle of their school day through the forest, hysterical to find my girl and give her an Easter hat kit when she already had one on her head. And so, with the teacher's prompt, I handed the bag to her reluctantly, feeling like I had totally let Cressy down. I quickly told her everything that was in the bag and begged her not to forget to give it to her.

Adam quite often picks the kids up, but that afternoon my work didn't seem to be quite so important. At 3 p.m., I grabbed the car keys and told him I'd do this one.

Deep down, I knew with my daughter's happy-go-lucky attitude, always looking out for how others felt, glass half full, little ledge personality, despite feeling totally guilt-ridden, this would really only go one way. She ran out of the gates with her arms out, screaming, 'Mummyyyyyy!' Oh God, that face. Elated. Beaming. Her school bag, an Easter bonnet and two extra carrier bags in hand.

'Did you have a wonderful day?' I asked. 'Did you get the stuff I brought in? I'm sorry I couldn't get it to you before you went Easter egg hunting. I tried my best.'

'Don't worry, I know you did. But I got everything and my friends were so happy when I said I had little chocolate eggs to share. It was so much fun. Thank you, Mummy.'

No problem, sweetheart. It was a piece of p*ss.

*   *   *

The teachers put up a beautiful end-of-term video and sent a YouTube link to parents. Eagerly, I get Adam to put it on the TV. Anything the school creates of these sweet kids is always so angelic and charming and the atmosphere they create with slow mo and music added is always impressive, so I was impatient to say the least ... Until I read the caption: 'Our Easter Fun'. I genuinely couldn't wait to watch it, for all of the reasons above, but it was tainted with the surge in anxiety of maybe seeing my little girl having no Easter bonnet, although deep down I knew they wouldn't show that. But what if I could see her disappointed face in the background? I would deal with it. But surely the school would look at the background before posting? Like, look at everything just in case a grown-up had screwed up. Which they sort of knew one had. Was I overthinking this? Jesus, just enjoy it, Ra.

We settled down on the sofa in PJs and a fluffy blanket, hot chocolate in hand. And then we asked the kids if they wanted to join us.

It was going fine. The start was beautiful. Little snippets of the day in the forest, with daffodils around them, laughing and frolicking among the woodland ... in their bonnets. I mean, not that I'm getting cold sweats at the very sight of a bonnet or anything, but did they have to put so much onus on them? Or maybe they didn't. Sh*t, yeah, they are literally just wearing them. Calm down.

The longer it goes on, the more extravagant the Easter bonnets get. I'm sure I just saw one that is the exact replica of what Helena Bonham Carter wears as the Queen of Hearts in *Alice in Wonderland*. Seriously? I mean, it's a masterpiece. I'm both in awe of how amazing it is and p*ssed off by the fact that teachers may think the kid had anything to do with it. I swore I would never be this parent. Who's worried? Not me.

The good news is, whatever I was feeling about my inadequacy, Cressy hadn't noticed. Watching it, her eyes were alight. She was mentioning every person's name in the video; she was talking about her best friend Bella, she said what a lovely person that boy was, how kind that girl was and then she said, 'You know what was funny though, Mummy?'

'No. What, darling?'

'The Easter Bunny had exactly the same curly hair as our teacher coming out of the back.'

And there it was. In hysterics, all was right with the world.

LIFE LESSON
ACCORDING TO CLARA BATTEN: 5

DON'T DO ANYTHING YOU'RE MEANT TO ON TIME.

Fix a situation later and you will be seen as a hero.

'G' IS FOR 'GORGING' ...

Along with sleepless nights, nappy blowouts and toddler negotiations, A&E dashes are another parental rite of passage. If you haven't done a panicky jump in the car and whizzed your child off to hospital only to have it turn out, after a six-hour wait, that they're absolutely fine, then you're probably doing something ... erm, right.

Monty has a very high temperature of 39.9. We kept an eye on him, tried to keep him cool and gave Calpol until his doctor's appointment at 4 p.m. At one point he started to look weird, not making a lot of sense. His eyes rolled and his head dropped; he was almost floppy. Absolutely petrified, I desperately needed to get him to help asap. I ran to him and picked him up, shouting to Adam in his office that we needed to take Monty to hospital. We got in the car and I sat in the back with our son, talking to him all the way to try and keep him mildly alert. Not knowing what was wrong was the most frightening of all. But also knowing that when your brain overheats and it starts affecting your speech and consciousness, it's extremely concerning. Well, not 'knowing' this – I'm guessing. But I wouldn't have thought going floppy was ideal for any living being. I was trying not to hyperventilate, myself – I was that worried. We just needed to get him there. And quickly.

To be fair to the staff, although there was a wait because, well, it's A&E, it wasn't the usual two-hour mundane linger on plastic chairs, which, no matter when we go, what circumstance we are in, what day of the week it is, inevitably ends in a numb arse.

Diagnosis: an ear infection. Apparently, a high temperature in a child can cause dehydration and heat exhaustion and make them feel extremely sick. I mean, don't get me wrong, I was ecstatic that's 'all' it was. But really? An ear infection made him literally look like he was about to die. I think the human body should kindly know what will give mothers a minor heart attack and not actually let it ever look that bad unless it IS that bad.

This is a problem for us as parents. Anything is a massive worry. I'm not talking colds or coughs, but when something's out of the ordinary, your child is more than a little rundown and you can tell something isn't quite right, our minds go into overdrive and start thinking the worst. You start on the 'what ifs', wondering how and what could ease their suffering. And apparently this never stops. Even when the child is my age, so my mum tells me. Oh, goodie. A lifelong period of parent anxiety. What fun.

*   *   *

Easter holidays, it is. I'm really looking forward to spending more time with the kids. I actually love family time, particularly at Christmas, Easter and on birthdays. There's something to be said for these events being way more exciting once you have kids. You remember what it was like when you were a child. I'm one of those mums (actually, I think most of us are) who can get overly enthusiastic about an Easter Egg hunt or dressing up as an elf (yeah, I've never done that, but I want to), purely because of the genuine excitement it conjures up in our kids. Before I had children and after I had finished being one (you know, sort of) these occasions were missing a little magic. And by magic, I mean lies.

Let's be honest, because we aren't honest when it comes to this. Easter and Christmas are only so magical for kids because of the lies we tell them. Santa Claus and a rabbit deliver millions of gifts to kids around the world overnight. Yeah, of course. I consider Cressy and Monty to be pretty intelligent for their age. They question where that coin actually was when I pretend to take it from behind their ear. But when I say nine reindeer are going to fly up into the sky dragging a massive bloke on a big sledge, with enough presents for the whole world in it and deliver all of them within 12 hours, there's not a doubt in their minds. I prefer to think this is a sign of a greater interest in fantasy than a sign of greater gullibility. Either way, this is the only big lie I'm willing to tell them. And it's a pretty massive one considering it's told annually for the first decade of their life. But I literally don't bat an eyelid at it. In fact, I probably go overboard with it.

There are quite a few articles, 'studies' and reports on the argument that we should not tell our children that Santa or the Easter Bunny exists. I read them a while back when I was pregnant with my first, as I was interested, after overhearing a woman in a café (always a café, never the queue to KFC. Mums are always having a coffee or a Perrier water in a café. I've never overheard any parenting advice by standing behind someone ordering a Bacon and Egg McMuffin. In fact, I'm pretty sure I actually ventured out of my London flat to a café many times, purely to pick up some free parenting advice when I was heavily pregnant with my first, on maternity leave, and had sod-all else to do. Oh, how I miss those days!).

I digress. Said woman was telling her friend she would always tell the truth about Father Christmas, so I thought I should just have a listen for 36 minutes at the different views she had, even though I knew with 100 per cent conviction that those fake snow, icing-sugar Santa foot-prints through our living room would continue long into the future.

I mean, what impact can a Christmas fantasy have on our children's relationship with us, other than suddenly being distraught at the thought of something they believed in was just elaborate deceptions being told time and time again by the people they trust most?

Oh, hang on …

In my extensively broad research on this topic, which consisted of typing into Google, 'lying to children about Father Christmas', one of the first articles that came up was titled: DON'T TELL CHILDREN FATHER CHRISTMAS IS REAL BECAUSE LYING TO CHILDREN COULD DAMAGE THEM, WARN EXPERTS (Credit: *Independent*). 'Warn experts' … Well, those experts don't cut the mustard with me, I'd rather go by experience.

Anyway, the article goes on to say: '*Psychology professor Christopher Boyle and social scientist Dr Kathy McKay also condemn the idea of a "terrifying" North Pole intelligence agency which judges children to be nice or naughty.*'

TERRIFYING NORTH POLE INTELLIGENCE AGENCY? Give me a bloody break. Next, you'll be telling me rewards for good behaviour or reward charts are us waving a finger in their face at how atrocious they are the rest of the time. Never have my kids felt 'terrified' by the thought that Santa and his elves were sitting in their toy factory scheming to punish their behaviour. Actually, maybe I should check on that. Even when told that Father Christmas is pleased they've been so good and can't wait to give them presents (knowing they haven't 'been good the whole time'), they still understand being good and working hard at things normally brings praise and 'rewards' in many senses of the word. Surely, this is the PERFECT life lesson to teach your child?

Right, that's enough internet for one day.

* * *

I have a cold. Sickness, shivering, aching all over, sensitive to the touch. But I don't think I have the flu, or, ahem, Covid. If my husband had one symptom from the above list, that would be it. Game over and zero chance of it being anything but the flu.

We have all seen it, though. We have. And genuinely, this is not just women being dicks about men. This is reality. And not to generalise, but let me quickly generalise. If a woman has a viral infection/cold/cough, etc., ON THE WHOLE she'll go about her normal day and maybe mention it to a friend in passing. Men will fuss about it, bang on about it, feel like it's getting in their way, mention details of how they can't stop sneezing, or how watery their eyes are. They get frustrated or irritable that they have to deal with it, stay in bed longer, excessively shiver. I mean, this is what I've heard. It's something like that. I haven't seen it myself. Really. Apparently, it's called 'Man Flu' or something like that. Disclaimer: I *have* seen it. I've seen it with my own eyes, in my own house.

My main concern about being unwell is that I won't be able to run. Yes, we're still doing that running every day for 100 days malarkey. Boring, isn't it? But look, it's all for the children, so I'm afraid you're going to have to put up with little snippets of the journey. I say 'journey' both in a metaphorical *and* a completely literal sense, you know, with it being 100 BLOODY MILES.

Anyway, I feel like utter crap. Really terrible. The first time I have actually felt ill (as in not having a cold (men)) in about three years and I'm damned if it's going to get in the way of this run today. We have already had to stop and then start all over again because of a swamp and I refuse for this to happen again on Day 45. NO WAY.

OK, so historically, people who follow me and watched my charity running videos on TikTok have loved it when I have found days tough. When I've cried in the rain in the dark. When I've been injured and unsure if I could carry on. When I say people 'have loved it', I don't mean they're complete psychopaths who sit there rubbing their palms together slowly, watching the clip over and over again, getting off on my struggles, waiting for me to mess up. I mean, they love them, as in these videos do well, going by the sheer number of views they clock up. Oh, wait … My followers are psychopaths.

My motivation to get out there and run was going to be my struggle today. That sounds very weird. I'm struggling, but struggling means more video views. More video views means the algorithm sends the videos out to more people. More people viewing means more donations to the NSPCC.

Feeling horrendous just putting on my leggings, shaking, head pounding, eyes aching. But I mustered up the stamina to go downstairs. It was a mild day but overcast and crap, and I was freezing. Hoodie over my running top it had to be. I got out there.

I had started my vlog of today's run from my bed, then showed people how I felt at the start of the run. I told them I just needed to get it out of the way but without getting sicker, so I would be doing a slow jog. Because apparently if you go out running as a normal jog when you're ill, you can become really ill as a result but if you go out as a slow jog when you're ill, you come back exactly the same, if not a little better. Hmm ...*

It was really tough. Laborious. I did it, but got very tearful. Hey, who cares? My psychopathic followers will love it and therefore we will receive more money for the children who need it.

Upstairs, back on my bed, I search TikTok sounds for emotional music. Whack that over the top and bam! All ready to go. Post. There you go, you lunatics.

*   *   *

Good Friday. I was asked the other day what I thought the hardest part of parenting was. I'd have to say, it's definitely the kids.

So, Easter. I'm happy for my kids to eat chocolate eggs at Easter and not have the full understanding of why, or what the egg symbolises. What should I say? 'Hey, Cressy, stop scoffing those chocolate eggs a minute, while I explain something to you. You must know, the eggs that you're eating ... Well, not those ones, in fact no chocolate ones ... other ones were adopted by early Christians as a symbol

---

* I so hope sarcasm comes across on paper; this would usually be where I would do a side glance/eye roll in a video. 👀

of the resurrection of Jesus Christ. Jesus' resurrection is symbolised through the hard shell of the egg, but a normal egg, which represents the tomb in which He was buried. And the emergence of the chick (not from chocolate ones, by the way), which breaks through the shell, represents Jesus, who conquered death.'

Cressy, mouth full of chocolate: 'Mmmmm, yeah, Jesus. Yeah, He died to save things. Us. Yeah, great. I'm very thankful. Can I have a caramel one?'

Well, that's how I imagine it would go anyway. Maybe I'll try it next year.

Some will say, well yes, you SHOULD explain. I didn't REALLY know why eggs were significant at Easter. And I learnt Christianity at school. For crying out loud, I took RE GCSE a year early! I got it. You know, the premise of Easter. But I certainly didn't put two and two together with the chocolate egg scenario because, let's be honest, there really isn't one. Just another bloody excuse to indulge. And I quite like that. Mainly for selfish chocolate-related reasons.

It wasn't until Easter Saturday (Is it called Easter Saturday? Oh, sh*t. Please, any devout Christians, please don't come for me. I'm sorry, I'm rubbish. It's the Saturday before Easter Sunday) that I realised what a rubbish parent I can sometimes be.

I have Nana's Easter eggs ready for the children. Oh yes, they've been here in Daddy's study for two days. Two beautiful Easter eggs from Nana and plenty of small ones to hide in the garden ... all from Nana. Grandma and Grandpa even sent some from up north and put 'fragile' on the outside (which actually worked, as they're not smashed to pieces). But don't you worry, I'm about to go to Tesco to get the lamb and two Easter eggs for my children. I've not left it too late. I remember Easter eggs being sold at half price days after Easter. Ones they needed to get rid of. Ones that hadn't been sold, so I was maybe even going to get a discount on these ones, being 4 p.m. the day before Easter. That would be a result. I got to Tesco: the Easter egg shelves were bare. WHAT?! I politely asked a member of staff to check out the back.

'No, I'm sorry. We know there aren't any there because we sold out about six hours ago.'

'I'm sorry? Who buys their kids Easter eggs days in advance?'

'Quite a lot of people.'

'Could you just check anyway?'

Why do we do this? We know it's going to waste their time and ours and only make the waiting time that more boring, twiddling thumbs, pondering the next move.

'As expected: nothing.'

And in true British form: 'I'm so sorry to have wasted your time. Do you happen to know where else might have them in stock?' I mean, at this point I'm presuming all Tesco workers are a walking encyclopaedia of stocklists of Easter eggs for every retail shop within a two-mile radius.

'To be honest, we heard of one customer who went to the big Asda in Eastbourne today and they were even sold out. And that's 40 minutes away. She was obviously on a mission.'

'Thank you. I have an idea.'

I remembered that when everyone was bulk buying in the height of the pandemic and all supermarkets had sold out of Calpol, the only place I could get it was at the BP petrol station shop, right on my doorstep. I headed straight there. Again … bare shelves. It was now 5.30 p.m. the day before Easter and I had no Easter eggs for my children from their parents. I know, the corner shop. Oh yes, fabulous idea, Clara. Let's try the only shop run by people who don't celebrate Easter. But I didn't care – I was willing to give anything a shot.

As the bell on the door rang as I flung it open, I said in the most flustered manner, 'Hello. I know you don't do Easter per se, but do you have anything like eggs, which are not eggs which you cook? Like, not ones from chickens. Other ones. Chocolate. Toys. Any eggs?'

What the hell was I saying?

'Well, yes. We have those toy ones there. We have Peppa Pig ones and Paw Patrol ones, and of course Kinder Eggs.'

'You legends, I could kiss you!'

I've never bought so many eggs of so many different sizes which resembled so many other things other than Easter eggs. I jumped in the car feeling very smug. And relieved that the kids would only have a sugar high for 90 per cent of the day.

*   *   *

Easter Sunday, here it is. The day we gorge on chocolate eggs and spring lamb. Everything which, if you think about it, makes you feel a bit sh*t about what you're doing, but by the same token in love with it all. How is that? Let's not dwell on it.

I've noticed a running theme on social media since part of it is sort of my job. On days like Christmas, Easter, holidays, birthdays, in-the-house days, out-in-the-garden days, laying around days – in fact, any damn days – there's a sort of perfection to 'adhere' to. But not everything – in fact, hardly anything – is perfect. I see a lot of big social media creators using their platform to teach people to be real and show us in our true form, our real life, warts'n'all and I absolutely love that. There's ways of doing it too, which can be extremely humorous and massively relatable.

There is one account, however, which I sincerely believe doesn't ever have to work hard to create perfection in her photos as there would physically not be enough time in the day to do what she does AND take random photos of her house, garden, fires and animals looking so good if they didn't already look like this. I present to you @mymidhurstlife. Now I don't get jealous of many people's lives but, by God, her house is immaculate, but not the crap immaculate, with no character. In a very down-to-earth sort of crappy, immaculate bloody sodding way. Oh, I can't explain it. Besides, I'm sure it won't be quite as thrilling to you as it is me. But it has been a running joke between us that when Christmas, or Valentine's, or Easter comes about, I put a video of her set-up up with the tagline 'Expectation' and then my very different set-up with the tagline 'vs Reality'. It's quality comedy content. Bloody hilarious. And definitely never been done before. OK, you have to be there, you have to see it. And actually, even then it still probably isn't that funny. Yeah, it sounds positively rubbish but I quite enjoy it.

Perfect or not, I am very much looking forward to hiding eggs in the garden (thanks, Nana) for the kids to find now that they're of an age where it's going to be remembered and enjoyed that much more. I'm a very emotional person. I cry at documentaries, at adverts, at *Britain's Got Talent* (I mean, if it happens to be on, you know, when I walk into the living room and accidentally tread on the remote control and press ITV bang on 8 p.m. Yeah, then). Goddammit, I used to cry at *Neighbours*. So it's unsurprising that I welled up a bit today, seeing Cressy and Monty's little faces when I told them a rabbit, with no opposable thumbs, had literally picked up many chocolate eggs and dumped them quite strategically around their garden. Not just on the grass at their own rabbit height, but at all sorts of inappropriate altitudes and balanced on branches no one in their right mind could conceive of any rabbit doing. But this, in that moment, and for the next hour, it seems, was in fact particularly believable.

That's enough about Easter. I ate a shed-load of lamb and duck-fat roast potatoes, there were some vegetables, a lot of cheesecake and even more chocolate ... and booze.

The diet's going brilliantly, thanks for asking.

'O' IS FOR 'OPPORTUNITIES'...

Obviously I love seeing Cressy and Monty's faces light up when they come in from school and are greeted by the other parent who didn't pick them up, and I love the gathering of chocolate eggs together from around our garden, but when they're at school what I would love to do all day, every day, is act. Be an actress. Sorry, and write books. HarperCollins: I, Clara Batten, bloody LOVE writing books. *Promise.* And by 'all day, every day', I mean exactly that. Literally. I would be absolutely fine to come home and give the kids a story once Adam has done the nightmare part: supper, bath, PJs, teeth. Really, I'd be fine with it. We all would be, if we're honest. Even though two hours of compromises, negotiations, nagging and tantrums is one of the things I look forward to most in my day, some nights I really wouldn't mind if our children just threw a spanner in the works and got ready for bed, read a story with us in under 13 minutes, said a chirpy goodnight, walked into their bedrooms and hopped into bed without a fuss. Honestly, if they stirred things up a bit and gave that a whirl, that would be A-OK – I actually quite like surprises.

I have to gear myself up for the evening stint after supper. After some downtime, I say, 'Five more minutes then we're going upstairs.' Five minutes goes by and they're happily chilling in front of their iPads. I am also very chilled. Surprisingly so. Might pour myself a gin and tonic. Why would I want to change this situation? So, all of a sudden, after five minutes, they are given three minutes more, but they think it's still part of the original five minutes. Those three minutes come and then go and normally another six or seven before I say, 'Right, two minutes,' when in fact we are already 14 minutes into the five minutes I initially gave them. At this point, they aren't doing anything wrong but I, as the parent, am the one quite literally using the delaying tactics I so often tell them not to, so that I can savour this peace and put off the dreaded bedtime 'routine'. I tell you now, this hasn't been close to a 'routine' since they were about eight months old. Those were the days of bubble machines and duckies in the bath every evening while I sang nursery rhymes to them and put bubbles on their head to 'Pampers ad' giggles. Gone are the days of brushing teeth while they sit in their baby bath seat with a chewable toothbrush in their mouth, followed by a swaddle in bath towels, a calm lie-down on the bed while I blow raspberries on their tummies, put their jammies on and read them a bedtime story which involves three words per 'touchy-feely' sensory page and takes 23 seconds to get through. Now, they're lucky if they get more than a Sunday night bath and a token mid-weeker.

Our current evening 'routine' is as follows:

Step 1. A getting-up-the-stairs contest, which undoubtedly ends in the 'loser' pretending to cry or having an actual paddy about it 'not being fair';

Step 2. A hoo-ha over which flavour of toothpaste they want, followed by a takeover of the brushing halfway through by a parent (unfortunately not any parent, normally one of us);

Step 3. A petty argument over whose turn it is to choose the bedtime story and then 12 interruptions during the reading of said story;

Step 4. Five minutes of using me as a human climbing frame while I rapidly flip the pages of the book;

Step 5. A goodnight 'make-up hug' between siblings while they whisper a planned alliance to delay bedtime;

Step 6. A seven-minute game of hide and seek I didn't know we were playing and about £8 lost in negotiations to a pre-schooler and a four-year-old;

Step 8. Sofa and *Gogglebox*. I mean, The History Channel.

* * *

Adam had his 40th and 41st birthdays in lockdown, so when I turn 40 in August we're going to have a joint party to make up for it. We have sent out 'save the date' texts and hope to be able to have a big bash in the field next to our garden. I don't want to sound like a wannabe hippy at one with nature, but we're thinking tepees or a small marquee. Fire pits. Live music. And by that, I mean some random boyfriend of someone I've invited bringing a barely tuned acoustic guitar and strumming it while we all sit around a campfire and sing 'California Dreamin' or 'Hotel California'. Basically, anything with the word *California* in it. Food: maybe a hog roast, although everyone's vegetarian or vegan nowadays, particularly hippies (sweeping generalisation), so in fact we definitely couldn't be bohemian types. All that is to say, I'm trying not to think about the fact that we will have to cater for dairy-free, lactose-free, gluten-free pescatarians, vegetarians and vegans – all things I'm pretty sure never existed in 1981 when I was born.

Some people worry about milestone birthdays but, as I get older, I find myself worrying less about them. I remember being so excited about my 21st birthday but then also thinking, 'Oh my God, I'm properly in my twenties. My teens are way out of sight now,' and again turning 30. It seemed that much older than my late twenties, but then I wasn't married by the time I was 30, which was just horrific; or engaged, even worse, and I certainly hadn't had my first child, which was definitely the biggest part of my teenage lifeplan.

Bottom line is though, I always thought, the single life in London in my twenties, with a good job, a cool flat, great friends, dates with city boys, trendy bars (not dates *with* trendy bars, I just went to a few), good restaurants, going to comedy gigs, crazy nights and day drinking on a sunny Sunday by the river was going to be the highlight of my life, the ultimate in 'living'. You know, being in one of the greatest cities in the world, young, free and single, these would be the stories to tell my grandchildren. But, then, I would need to have children first in order to tell those grandchildren my stories. But, of course, I certainly do have the stories to tell. Sod it, let's give you one. Don't get too excited …

My friend Becs had a birthday party once. Probably more than once. But this particular birthday party is not one she had planned. It was early on in our friendship, probably about 16 years ago. Let's just say those were our 'reprobate days' … OK, reprobate *years*.

Background: her boyfriend when I first met her was good friends with my brother, Ben, and the two of us never even met in the two years of them going out because that boyfriend told my brother it would be 'chaos'. Needless to say, we eventually met at my brother's birthday and from then on it was, as he had rightly predicted, chaos.

So anyway, for her birthday, her then boyfriend had taken the time to plan a party (not the one who didn't want to introduce us, a later one. I'm finding it hard to keep up myself and I've just started. I would use names to make it easier but I fear I might be taken to court. Let's call this one Dave – now I really MIGHT be taken to court).

It was a surprise party at a bowling alley, on a Saturday afternoon. He stole her phone for contacts of past and present colleagues she may or may not want there. He also messaged all of her close friends and mutual friends of them both and set up an afternoon of bowling, drinks and, for some, food. (Bloody hell, do you remember, pre-pandemic, when we used to put three fingers into a bowling ball and then, quite literally, eat pizza, burgers and nachos with those same three fingers seconds later? Good times.)

The night before her party, we had a wine-fuelled night and she told me that she hoped her boyfriend didn't have anything planned. Although she's the life and soul of any party, surprises are not her thing. Myself and our friend Jaimie were keeping quiet while her boyfriend texted to say he hoped she wasn't going mad tonight as it was her birthday tomorrow. We did go mad that night and, after a lot of coaxing from Becs, I still said, 'No, I really don't think he has anything planned but, um, if he did, what would you ideally like to do? Like, any ball games, or ...?'

'No, mate, what the f*ck?! I'd like to go to a pub near my flat, like this one, get a gin and tonic and a bottle of white, maybe eight or nine packets of pork scratchings and wash them down with a tequila or two.'

Jaimie interrupted: 'Oh, for f*ck's sake, if you really want to know, he has bowling planned somewhere I've barely heard of in the middle of the business district somewhere.'

'Are you kidding me?'

'Look, mate, it's not that bad,' I said with a sarcastic glint in my eye. 'It will only take 45 minutes on the tube, which you're no longer allowed to drink on, and it's booked for about 1 p.m. so you won't be able to have your usual lie-in after tonight. And you'll probably feel sick. And look sh*t. Oh, and it's a surprise, with loads of people you may not have seen for a while. And still don't want to see. But other than that, it's going to be a blast.'

She didn't look sh*t at all. In true form, she got herself together and made the effort. She dressed up, hair blow-dried to perfection, she pretended she had no idea, surreptitiously drank a few cans of piña colada on the tube, looked surprised when we got there, took a few shots – at the bowling pins as well – and actually quite enjoyed herself. I was loving it, high on life and doing shots at the bar with her ex-work colleagues, who probably had names like Janet and Sylvia. I have no idea. But after the previous night and having had very little to eat at the bowling alley, bar some cocktail sausages and mini-vol-au-vents, like I was in 1984, I took myself out for some fresh air. And by fresh air, I mean a Marlboro Light, on a busy London street, where I could barely see the cigarette in my hand for fumes. Or drinking too much. One of the two anyway.

I knew it was time to leave so I jumped in the nearest taxi before anyone could see I had left the venue. It had been a crazy night and I just needed my bed.

'What's the time, please?' I asked the cab driver

'Three o'clock.'

'In the morning?' I asked, shocked.

'No, in the afternoon.'

F*ck me. I didn't know whether to be disgusted with myself that I had lasted two whole hours at the party, or elated and proud that I would be tucked up in bed with a Chinese takeaway by 5 p.m.

As we pulled up to my flat and I sifted through my wallet to find some cash, the taxi driver gave me a very weird look.

'Are those bowling shoes?' he asked.

SH*T.

'Erm, yes.'

There was a moment which seemed to last about five minutes when we both continued to look at the shoes, then at each other and then back at the shoes again. For some reason, I was trying to think of an excuse as to why I had them, as if he was the CEO of Hollywood Bowls, who ironically probably wouldn't give a monkey's if I had them or not.

'I'm borrowing them for a bowling tournament tomorrow and then I'll take them back and get my own shoes, which I have left as a deposit.'

'OK, I don't care. Card or cash?'

Going into my flat, I was very upset. I had left my favourite 'cavegirl'-style boots at the bowling alley. Ones I wore 80 per cent of the time. Going back to get them seemed akin to climbing Mount Everest and was not an option. I called the bowling alley to let them know my boots were still there. Back then I was in sales and thought I was pretty damn hot at negotiation so what better way to test that theory out than on the phone to a 24-year-old ten-pin bowling receptionist after two porn star martinis, a bottle of wine and a couple of shots of tequila?

'I will not be able to come back. Firstly, your establishment is in a weird faraway place, which even now I still don't think I have any idea what it is called.'

(Doing well so far.)

'Well, it's in …'

'Really, it doesn't matter. I won't be coming. I have an excellent idea. Will you do me a small favour?'

'Yes, no problem.'

'I'm going to order a taxi. If you could just run upstairs and pop my boots in the cab for me, that would be great.'

'Are you kidding me?'

'Don't worry, I'll pay for the cab.'

'Yeah, that's not what I was worried about. No!'

'Sorry, I'll have to take your first answer of "Yes, no problem".'

I never DID get those boots back. Couldn't manage the journey. But it did mean I was the proud owner of some retro bowling shoes which I was hoping might be worth some money one day but at the very least proved very comfortable on nights out and a great ice-breaker for conversations, if not a tad out of place.

Every cloud ...

So there, you see. It was *wild*.

Another best friend of mine – Rob – and I also had some slightly uncivilised times in our London days. We were both living in the home counties at the time but would meet in central London for a night out. He was my brother's good friend at uni and we had recently met again at Ben's wedding after a decade and hit it off. We met up often after that: we talked about everything, we laughed till we cried, we visited each other's family homes and some-times argued like brother and sister. I wasn't quite sure what our relationship was – really, we just kissed when we'd had a bit to drink. We used to have these riotous nights out, miss our trains home and then get a hotel for the night. These weren't glamorous hotels, I might add. We would purposefully get the tube to a cheaper part of town, like King's Cross was back then, and get a skanky £40-a-night job. Inevitably though we would end up sleep-ing fully clothed; with him, I'm certain, sleeping with one eye open. But I wasn't going to make the move. Maybe it was the unpleasant hotels we were staying in, or perhaps it was something else, but as soon as we were on our own it was a 'Goodnight' and a roll over. Now I don't want to sound like one of those girls who says, 'He didn't even crack on, he must be gay,' but he didn't even crack on.

'He must be gay,' I thought.

Not because people can't resist me, just because I've been around enough men after they've had a few drinks.

Anyway, one night we were at a swanky private members' club. We were on track to get our trains back home but, as I was leaving, I was introduced to Robbie Coltrane (RIP) and the evening carried on. A few of us joined him and his friends for a drink at a very prestigious hotel. I had definitely missed my train, but then Heath Ledger (RIP again. Not everyone who meets me ends up this way) turned up p*ssed (I'm aware this sounds made up, it's not) and as I was trying to negotiate getting the last room (which was way out of my price bracket, but Robbie offered to put it on his 'tab'), Rob called to say he had missed his train too. I selflessly gave the last room to Heath Ledger (now there's a sentence I never thought I'd say) and headed back to the club to meet Rob. We had a glass of prosecco, a cheeky drunken snog and booked one of the rooms there. Smart hotel, four-poster bed, romantic lighting …

'If this doesn't do it, nothing will,' I thought.

I went to the bathroom to freshen up. I heard the TV go on and as I walked out with a girly giggle, I saw Rob under the covers, shirt buttoned up to his collar, snoring like a train. I lay on the bed, opened a can of beer from the minibar and looked up at the TV. Late-night Jerry Springer was on and the title 'My Ex's Mistress is Now My Girlfriend and We're Raising His Daughter' was plastered along the bottom of the screen. I spotted the remote on the bedside table on Rob's side. There was no way I was moving. I was destined to watch trashy American TV for the next 45 minutes purely because I just couldn't be arsed to move.

The next morning, as usual, we got up as best mates and slipped back into the platonic banter we always had and actually both knew was the best thing for us. Mainly because he was gay ... In my mind, anyway. We decided to go for lunch. It was a beautiful summer's day and we sat in a charming beer garden in leafy south-west London, not caring that we were still in the same clothes from the night before. We ordered tapas-style starters to share and a bottle of rosé. Rob had said that he needed to charge his phone so I said I would plug it in inside when I went to order our mains. As I plugged it in, it lit up and the first thing I saw was his recent text from a few minutes previously: 'It went really well. I think I like him a lot.' I put it down, as I didn't want to read the private text messages of my best friend. He could surely tell me anything, at his own pace.

I called my mum quickly and told her I was certain he was gay and wanted him to be able to talk to me. She said, 'Well then, just ask him? And be there for him.'

I decided to bite the bullet.

'Rob, take off your sunglasses, I need to talk to you and see your eyes. Look, you know you're my best friend. I don't care about anything. Nothing bothers me. Nothing fazes me. And your happiness is paramount. Whatever you think or feel, I will always be there for you, 100 per cent. You know that, right?'

'You're scaring me with your seriousness. But yes.'

'So, please just know you can talk to me. I love you as my best mate and I want you to know you can talk to me about anything. OK, so … In my heart of hearts, Rob, I think you … I think you're gay. Please know that you can be honest with me.'

There was a pause.

'Is it because I'm drinking pink wine, have frosted tips in my hair and occasionally wear fake tan?'

'Well, no. But now you say *that* …'

We both cracked up and amid the laughter he said, 'No, I'm not, Ra, you muppet! Really!'

So, I left it at that. All in his own time.

And it turns out, his own time was nine years later at the age of 38.

He's always been one of a kind. The warmest, funniest guy anyone could have in their life. I am utterly proud to have him (and his fiancé Tom) as godfathers to Cressy. And relieved that all those times I doubted myself, he was totally gay and had he been straight he just may well have cracked on. Maybe …

All jokes aside, it was an amazing period. I look back on those London times as brilliant fun but the truth is I also remember feeling a bit empty, like something was missing. London in your twenties could also be a bit stressful. I was often hungover, dating, between various jobs and trying to figure out what I loved doing. In many ways, life's a lot simpler now, even though I have two lovely little ratbags to look after. I wish I'd backed myself a bit more back then, pushed myself harder, as it's taken having kids to make me realise how competent I actually am. I definitely think, why did I put up with that sh*t or sit around in that job that I didn't like as much as I should? I would have kicked a few boyfriends into touch sooner too. But on the upside, it's good to have got it all out of my system as at least I'm not living with real regret. These are First World issues of course, but you can see why lots of women make a success of whatever they do after having kids as, for a lot of people, it gives you the confidence to go out and do what you enjoy most and give it a good old go. And this is why I'm trying, in one of the most dog-eat-dog industries out there, to be an actress all over again at the grand old age of 40.

Sh*t, what the hell am I doing?

My thirties, and my late thirties at that, have been the most exciting and fulfilling years of my life in many ways. Even though it's been a tough and testing few years – what with the tiny matter of a global pandemic and Adam's business going down the pan – the past few years have taught me what is key to a happy life. There have been lessons learnt, changes in perspective, the realisation of what is important (TikTok). No, I'm kidding, but how time with family is precious and much needed for everyone. There are exciting times ahead. And way more exciting than the ones I thought were so exciting in my 'exciting twenties'.

I have never looked forward to the future as much as I do now. It's an odd concept to me that as I approach 40, the typical 'middle-aged age', I'm actually the most excited I've ever been to see what the next decade has in store. I'm eager to see things developing in my weird and crazy new 'career' (again, in the loosest possible sense of the word), to see whether it might become something close to acting. I'm so looking forward to mine and Adam's party, Cressy starting a new chapter come September, with Monty joining her school, us parents meeting more new school friends, having our first family holiday in years, actually getting down to writing the comedy series that my friend and I have been planning for years, watching the kids develop and become even bigger characters, starting to go to the kids' sports matches and sports days, dinner parties with friends, summer barbecues with family, walks on the beach, making my book into a film, winning an Oscar for it and thanking Jeremy Clarkson in my acceptance speech for writing the article which ultimately led to the publishers of this book getting in touch. Too far?!

*　　*　　*

As if by magic, I get another Instagram DM. I'm beginning to like this method of communication, even though it can be a bit of a lottery as to whether I actually see them or not.

A comedy commercial and film director has messaged to ask if I have an agent for booking, whatever that means. Alas it's not Richard Curtis, but beggars can't be choosers. I told him that I didn't have an agent for anything. He quickly told me he wasn't about to offer to be my agent. *Damn.* He then explained that he was a film director, but again quickly caveated the statement with the fact he wasn't about to offer me a potentially life-changing role. I mean, talk about dangling the carrot.

Would you mind, then, sir, kindly telling me what the hell you ARE going to do?

He said he wasn't sure, that he was just thinking out loud. That my stuff kept popping up on his feed and that he thought I was a good comedic actress and should probably audition for a couple of things coming up.

Done. I'm there.

He said, 'Let's jump on a call at some stage.'

'I'm available now,' I wrote. 'Or whenever. You know. I'm easy. Well, I'm not EASY. No casting couch ideas, haha.'

Jesus, Clara, shut up! Not too late to unsend that message. Sh*t. Read.

'Five o'clock your time good?' he wrote.

'My time? What, you in LA or something? Haha.'

'Yes.'

'Right ... Yes, of course. Five p.m. is great. Hear you then.'

What?!

I found myself pacing up and down my living room with sweaty palms in the 10 minutes leading up to the conversation. What if I messed it up somehow? Can you mess up a chat on the phone? I wasn't being interviewed or auditioned. Surely if I was just myself, talking normally, it would be fine. But would I talk normally? Debatable. It was the biggest opportunity I'd had in, well, forever, and so to me everything was riding on it. I hadn't felt this nervous since I was 17, walking into my A-level exams.

I got off the phone ecstatic. Buzzing. Beyond excited. I had relaxed as soon as we started talking and it turned out there just MIGHT be a glimmer of an opportunity. We spoke for about an hour. Much less awkward than my bloody messages. Great sense of humour. Very funny. Easy to get on with. Charming.

And the director was pretty cool as well.

Looks like I've got an audition for a Christmas movie coming out this year. Well, he said, 'I'm directing a Christmas film and we have a few parts still to cast. Mainly men, though. Let me talk to the casting directors about a possible audition.'

Same thing, right?

'C' IS FOR 'COURAGE' ...

I'm not a chef. I'm a ... No, I'm not 'an' anything. I cook, I love to cook. And one of my 'things' is to try and revive leftovers into something which tastes just as good the following day. That used to be via the microwave, but I have found a much more time-consuming and only slightly tastier way to resuscitate certain foods. Hear me out. I still think the microwave is a magnificent way to revive so many dishes. Who the bloody hell do I think I am?! Bolognese, for example. Curry. Yes! These things taste better the next day and you can simply heat them up in a microwave and they will be amazing. Yes, did you know you can simply put food in the microwave and heat it up? Maybe that should be another of my invaluable Life Lessons.™ I'll tell you something else. You won't believe this, but if you want a healthy snack, you can take a banana, peel it using your hands and eat the inside. Boom! Thank me later.

BUT. Potatoes. Any form. Give them a bit of TLC and they can taste just as amazing as the day before with one simple life hack: fry them. New potatoes, roast potatoes, chips from the fish and chip shop, mashed potatoes … anything. Trust me. Game changer.

I came across this dazzling method when … Well, I didn't come across it, I did it one day. In my late thirties. And I'm p*ssed off I didn't do it sooner. You remember when I told you I was taking that very 'long-winded McDonald's' to my mother's house and we had the 'incident' with the lack of Grand Big Macs? Well, I'll let you into a little secret: there was more than one occasion when I brought her McDonald's. I know that's hard to believe but anyway there was a running theme with these McDonald's deliveries: 'Ra, the chips are cold and quite soggy. I remember them being quite crunchy and hot, back in the day.'

Yes, you're right: our chat stinks.

Anyway, I began a mission to resuscitate these golden beauties. OK, anaemic bad boys. I went to my mother's kitchen, pulled out a frying pan, chucked some olive oil in it and whacked the fries in. Weirdly, although I know how to cook many dishes, as well as heat things in the micro-wave, I really doubted it would work. Did I have to deep-fry them to get them to perfection, or even half-decent for that matter? Hang on, if I can fry semi-boiled new potatoes cut in half and end up with sautéed potatoes, surely I can shallow-fry already-cooked McDonald's fries and end up with crispy versions? Anyway, it took three minutes and with a sprinkling of Maldon sea salt flakes, they were done. So, that's how I came to learn how to revitalise any potato dish, at 39 years old.

I do the same with roast potatoes. Ditto, chip-shop chips. And I know Maldon sea salt flakes may make me sound like a posh tw*t. But no, I choose where best to spend the extra few pence. I buy my clothes from Primark and Sainsbury's. I buy own brand ketchup and mayo, because I actually think it tastes better and it's cheaper. But the one affordable luxury everyone must invest in is Maldon sea salt flakes. Trust me. I took those fries, chucked them in Sainsbury's own brand olive oil and sprinkled them with higher-than-average priced, crystallised flakes of deliciousness and boom! Ronald McDonald, call my agent … When I get one.

*   *   *

If you were wondering what could possibly be 'courageous' about potatoes, I wouldn't have blamed you, but I felt a bit of levity was needed before what's about to follow. Sometimes in life, things happen that make it hard to think of anything else, even heating up potatoes. Recently, I heard that a lovely, vivacious girl I knew so long ago, who I hadn't been in much contact with since leaving school other than the odd social media message, had felt it was too hard to carry on. That there was no way out from how she felt. That it would be better if she were no longer here. And that breaks my heart. All I've been thinking about is how she must have felt to go through such pain, to leave behind two small girls. I have cried plenty. Talked to my daddy in the sky. Asked him to look after her. Just writing this, tears are streaming down my face. It pains me so much that people feel so desperate that this end seems their only solace.

When I was told, I immediately remembered she had sent me a DM earlier this year. Frantically I went back to the message to see if I had replied, worried for some reason that I may have disappointed if I hadn't. Not because I'm a big deal, but because if you write a message to ANYONE – friend, acquaintance, family member – if you don't receive a response, particularly when going through your own struggles, these things might add to them. I don't know. For whatever reason, I was concerned. I read the message from her: 'Thank you for making lockdown a bit easier.' I was so relieved that I had replied, thanking her for supporting me, saying I hoped she and her beautiful family were well. I don't know why, and maybe selfishly, I felt some sort of relief that I hadn't ignored her message. It's so true that you never know what someone else is going through. Either way though, all I can think about and have in my heart and thoughts are her close friends and family, who will obviously be feeling an unbearable sadness.

Rest in peace, dear girl.

Oh God, how to continue this without the normal stereotypes. Without sounding 'preachy'. But f*ck it, I'm going to say it. If you're struggling, please reach out and talk to someone. More people love you than you know. It can get better and it's not the end for you. There's so much help out there through family, friends and professionals and it's strong and courageous to ask for help. To talk. Absolutely no one wants to see you go down this route.

I'm in no way trying to compare our situations at all, but I have struggled with my mental health sometimes. Most of the time I'm fine but when it hits, it's mainly some anxiety and normally triggered by something. I'm lucky it has not become too debilitating for me and I was surprised to see how many other people I follow on social media (a lot of comedy people too) have felt the same at some stage. Right now, for example, I'm over-analysing, worrying about how much I have on. I've been feeling like this for a little while. It feels a bit like in my own head I just don't feel as happy about everything. I'm usually a 'cup half full' type of girl so this is annoying and very unusual. And something I recognise all of a sudden, that I have to rectify and redress. Sooner rather than later.

I'm sure quite a few of you have felt the same at some stage. Overwhelmed, like you don't know where to start, anxious, panicky, like the slightest thing could make you burst into tears, like you're needing to get everything done yesterday but can't sort your head out to even get the one thing you need to do today. These include the very simple things in life. God forbid, you don't need to be in a high-powered job, or writing a book or, um, trying to be an actress to feel like this. Just having housework on, collecting kids, arranging bills, worrying about a family member. But also, you don't even have to have *anything* on. Sometimes you just really need to take a step back and breathe.

There, I just said it: I need to take a step back and breathe. And within two seconds of recognising this, I've completely slowed down my typing. I've just realised how incredibly fast I was going even in my brain down to fingers on the computer. After feeling like this for a while, of crying at the slightest thing where I can't get my breath, of getting a tight chest when I think of everything I need to do, days of snapping when there was really no need, I decide I need to talk.

It's important to use a platform like social media for good, particularly if you've got a reasonably decent following, so I post a video saying I'm going to take a break. It took many attempts, but in the end I went with it and let myself be vulnerable. Besides, why shouldn't people see that even someone who always seems so happy, carefree and positive might sometimes struggle too or feel down or anxious? And if nothing else, it will give my more psychopathic followers some 'good-quality' viewing. I spoke to my doctor and as well as advising I take some anti-anxiety pills when the physical symptoms happen, he said he would like to officially sign me off any work for at least two weeks. Although I don't have anyone to answer to, it just gave me the nod that I can feel OK about taking this time off. In fact, it's more than OK: it is highly beneficial and not something to worry about. Because although writing this book sometimes *feels* like therapy, it will actually be put on shelves in Waterstones to be read by the general public for roughly £15.

I was overwhelmed by the number of people who reached out to me after I posted that video. I didn't realise just how many people were feeling, frankly, as sh*t as I was. I suppose it's unsurprising, given that mental health statistics are rising so dramatically and it's great that so many people started supporting each other in the comments section. That's when you realise social media has big positives as well as a few negatives. Four professional therapists also got in touch to offer me free sessions, which was just so sweet and generous, and so I genuinely believe it can only be a good thing to take one up on their kind offer. As I said earlier, one conversation can be life-changing.

Today I had a therapy session on a Zoom call with a lady called Sonia Grimes. It was so helpful. In between telling me to slow down and take a breath during the session, she gave me some brilliantly simple breathing exercises and an amazing peripheral vision technique, which worked extremely well twice in the session. She said the fact I sped up so much in our conversation talking about what I had on was reflective of how my mind and nerves were feeling and I needed to try and slow down when feeling this and stop, take some breaths or some fresh air before it worked itself into a panic attack. This also worked. After my sessions with Sonia, I feel like something has shifted.

*   *   *

Our 100 days of running have reached their finale and so far Adam and I have raised £26,600 for the NSPCC. We get the train to London in May to do our final mile, ending it on London Bridge. I have told people online they can come and support at the end. Unfortunately, when we committed to starting the 100 days of running again, I didn't think the end date through properly, so we end it mid-afternoon on a Wednesday near one of the capital's biggest commuter hubs. Finishing mid-week isn't ideal either, given people, like, work and stuff, so I wasn't holding my breath for a sea of familiar faces at the end. No matter: in my head, we would be scrambling for the finish line as hordes lined the banks of the River Thames, cheering on the success of completing such a challenge, champagne corks popping, a finish line tape held across the bridge and maybe a local Sussex news station there with a camera. In reality, it was a couple of local friends who popped out of their London Bridge offices to watch, Cressy screaming frantically, 'Go, Mummy and Daddy', Monty in his buggy as the actual finish line, my mum recording on her phone and a toast of thanks, congratulations and gratitude in the form of Costa coffee cups half-filled with prosecco.

But really, that was not the point. It was being documented on a live stream on TikTok with thousands of people tuning in along the way. And this WAS the point: to raise as much awareness for the cause and ultimately as much money as we could. The whole reason we were doing this. Not for praise or 'well dones'. And everyone was being incredibly generous with the final donations in the concluding 20 minutes of running. We both had inflatable costumes on and started at Moorgate, ending at London Bridge. I had two phones in my hand, one to edit a one-minute video of the final mile and the other to do the live stream.

In true Batten fashion, we get lost in the City of London while suited and booted people, clutching their briefcases in the finance district, go about their day, walking with purpose to their next meeting. Meanwhile, Adam is waddling along in a princess, sumo blow-up outfit doing a much better attempt at jogging than I am in my dinosaur blow-up costume, filming on two phones, commentating and tripping over my own laces. Although we're probably going less than two miles an hour, these costumes are extremely tiring. We get to the finish line, which is the double buggy and a small black and white finish line flag held by Cressy, and take a big swig from the prosecco-filled coffee cup. With hugs from my mum, children and friends and cheers from a few random strangers on the bridge, we end our 100 days of running and I break down in tears unexpectedly. Who am I kidding? Totally expected. I carry on the live stream, asking the viewers the grand total raised for the NSPCC. A few of them go off to check: we are at £30,500. Almost £4,000 more gained in the last hour and we have hit the £30k. I'm in proper tears by now, overwhelmed by people's generosity. I'm so happy and grateful to have got to do this with my partner in crime, my followers. No, kidding, Adam, my soulmate, my best buddy, who jumped on this when I suggested it.

'Yeah, although *I* suggested it,' he laughs.

Potato, po*tart*o ...

QUOTES BY CRESSY

That same night ...

Me: 'Cressy, please, let's just start going to bed nicely. I've said you can have two friends to Monty's birthday but you're playing up so much it might just have to be one.'

Cressy: 'Mummy, earlier you said I was your best friend in the whole world.'

Me: 'You are.'

Cressy: 'Well, this doesn't sound very much like what a best friend would say.'

'K' IS FOR 'KEEPSAKES' ...

Reader, I dyed my hair. Well, OK, I dyed my parting. I had dark roots. My photo shoot with *YOU Magazine* wasn't too far off and I couldn't get an appointment. When I say 'dark roots', that's wishful thinking. It's more of a two-inch salt and pepper look, but more salt than pepper and more four inches than two. So, I did what any normal middle-aged mum with little time on her hands and no experience in hairdressing would do. I have highlighted hair and therefore block colour would look very weird, so I reached for some kitchen foil and a chopstick and attempted to replicate the highlighted look for myself.

I don't know what convinced me that this would be a great substitute for the real thing. It quickly became apparent this weaving movement I'd seen the professionals do is most definitely not as easy as it looks. What I did was more of a tidal wave movement and not at all delicate or close to a highlight I had ever seen. More, a general brushing of hair-damaging bleach in a random fashion which would end up not only rather patchy, but very brassy in colour and extremely white in other areas, depending on how long it had taken to do each part. Hey, just call me Nicky Clarke! On the whole I was very unimpressed by my efforts. Almost to the point of some anxiety. I knew I had to do something to 'calm it down a bit'. A rose gold, semi-permanent hair dye would be the obvious choice in this predicament, I feel. But I don't need one that has succinct directions on how to use it and how long to keep it on as I won't take any notice of them. Instead, I'll make it up as I go along. I chuck the whole bottle on my head and saturate every last strand.

I had friends coming over for lunch in an hour. Adam was in London catching up with old friends – not friends he had known for a long time, just friends who were in their forties and fifties. It was a girlfriend's birthday and I had offered to host a celebratory lunch. However, I had stupidly forgotten that we had zero gin left in the house. Of course, they probably would have been fine with wine instead, but not to be able to offer these 'occasional gin drinkers' gin was out of the question. More importantly, though, I had forgotten to get my friend a birthday card. I sifted through our 'card drawer', which I thought might have at least one generic card in there that I could pass off as a 'Birthday Wishes' one. But unless she had recently acquired an obsession with dinosaurs or an enthusiasm for unicorns, the cards I had were not going to pass. At 'our age' we can get away with not giving a present to someone hitting a 'milestone birthday', but a card is just common courtesy.

I knew it'd only take me eight minutes to get to my local shop and back, and that I'd still just about have time to wash off the dye before they turned up. When I reach the shop, at a petrol station forecourt, the queue is snaking out of the door.

Great. Plenty of time for everyone to notice the tangle of wet pink hair atop my head and wonder why the hell a My Little Pony replica decided coming out like this was a good idea.

In the line, a woman in front of me does a double take.

I point to my hair: 'I know, it's ridiculous. Basically, I put some pink hair dye on my hair and I have some friends coming round for lunch and I forgot to get a birthday card for one of them and I thought it better to be washing this out of my hair when they arrived rather than being out getting a card.'

'Actually, I just realised I follow you on TikTok,' she said.

I offer a shamefaced thanks.

'But now you've brought attention to it, I'm sure your hair will turn out great.'

When I get back, I run upstairs with one aim in mind: getting this sh*t off my hair. Not that I'm that bothered, it's semi-permanent after all. It will wash out eventually and anyway, I rather like the colour rose gold. Except ... this resembles nothing of the sort. It's more a purply, cerise, very bloody bright pink. Zero gold in this whatsoever. I look like one of those troll toys that we used to have back in the eighties and nineties, because actually, having just looked closer, the actual condition of my hair is not dissimilar to that of those trolls either. Yet another brilliant decision made by me. Luckily, my friends are used to my ridiculous entanglements and barely mention it.

*   *   *

I put the hair dye instructions which I didn't use in a drawer. Just in case they have some useful information I might need to know at a later date – like how I might speed up the process of getting this pink out of my hair.

Do you have a DRAWER? Maybe you have a few. I have one in a sideboard in the dining room. It's a drawer I put school prospectuses in and a notepad with a few random pens, most that don't work and without lids, but I still put them back just in case they work next time (a bit like these instructions). OK, so it might have a few rogue batteries in it too, but let's not confuse this drawer with the kitchen one. You know, I think it's actually got a name too. Yes, that's it: 'the kitchen drawer full of random crap'. It's the 'odd, unmatched drinks coasters, Christmas cracker mini-screwdriver set, McDonald's ketchup sachets, Blu Tack, oversized tape measure, empty pack of plasters, old camera negatives and three photos from 1987' drawer. If you know, you know. And you KNOW.

So anyway, in my drawer I have two beautiful 'memory books', one for each child. Quick synopsis: these are books in which you write wonderful memories. The books prompt you to write funny things the kids have said that year, holidays or trips you've been on, ailments you've had, houses you've lived in, the kids' favourite things to eat, to play with. You get the picture ... Then, when you're out of the chaotic early years, you have a lovely keepsake that reminds you of how sleep-deprived you were, how close to insanity you felt at times and when your beloved offspring sprouted their first tooth. Delightful.

Now firstly, and I'm not the only one to say this and I won't be the last, there's a significant difference in how much effort you put into treasuring every milestone of your firstborn in comparison to your second one. Your second one ... meh, not so much. Hang on, hear me out. I actually collected the first curl of my second one. I remembered to do that. You see, brilliant mother. I'm actually not even sure Cressy got that. Probably because I didn't cut her hair, which also didn't grow in the first few years. Cressy's the firstborn and I'm pretty sure she got everything else.

Bottom line is though, the difference between the two is – unintentionally – massive. I saved her (Baby No. 1) wristband from the hospital, I saved her first scan, I saved the clip that falls off the belly button (eugh!), I saved her first babygro and hat she wore out of hospital. I put them all in a little box for her to look at when she was older and for us to reminisce over. It was new, it was exciting. It was the first fr*cking life we had brought into this world. I mean, that is HUGE!! Monty we love no less, but let's be honest, the second one, there just isn't the novelty factor anymore. OK, so we made another one, another whole human being. But I don't really have that much time to be collecting all the things to save. I literally just need to work out how I'm going to deal with two of them, one being a bloody newborn. Survival mode is all I'm thinking right now, not how I'm going to keep all these nostalgic pieces for some big reveal later on in life.

I'm not going to lie, Monty's wristband broke as we were leaving the hospital and we couldn't find it, which immediately brought the whole sentimental thing I was 'meant to do' to my attention. And I freaked out. I literally raced, new stitches in, bleeding into what can only be described as an adult nappy, exhausted from a three-day horrific labour with little to no sleep, shouting at my 19-month-old daughter down the hallway, to 'wait there with Daddy!' I was jogging down the ward for what seemed like the length of the whole hospital until I got to a midwife I recognised and realised I had moved about eight metres.

'Thank goodness I found you,' I said in a true, over-dramatic, hormone-filled way, 'Do you have a spare one of these?' (pointing to my own wristband) 'which you could write my son's name on? Don't worry about the rest of the info, I know you're overrun on the ward at the moment, but his sister has one so I want to be able to show it to him when he's a really unappreciative teenager who will most likely look at it, mutter "thanks" under his breath and walk out the front door.'

(NB: I don't know why I think my son's going to turn out to resemble Kevin or Perry.)

The midwife nodded with a sweet sympathetic smile, but I could see she was actually thinking, 'Just whatever you do, don't piss off this hormonal new mum who's been up for three nights straight in an induction, then in labour and then feeding her newborn baby through the night.' I walked out with a brand new, straighter-than-straight wristband, able to write what the hell I liked on there. This could be quite fun ... And possibly very immature. But I'm alright with that and hopefully he will be too, given the fact that the law of averages suggests he might have a mildly OK sense of humour by the time I give it to him on his 18th birthday (yes, it will be in front of all his mates).

My point being, it's actually OK that this happens. The whole second child thing. Monty's babygros were always passed down to him and he DOES have his belly button thing. Which is pretty gross, come to think of it. But we forgot about keeping his first dummy, so bought a newborn one when he was three months old and chucked that in the box. We also went back to print off an earlier scan from a CD as we lost his first scan in our house move. We then whacked it all in a cleaned-out Chinese takeaway box. Not the foil ones with the cardboard lid, that would be so wrong. But one of those plastic see-through ones with the cutout holes in the top so the steam can get out and the food doesn't go soggy.

Those ones.

So, these memory books. These books, you fill them in every year up until they're 18. This seemed like a very good idea at the time when I had my first newborn baby sleeping 18 hours a day, no work, except looking after a little baby, taking numerous photos of her and savouring every moment. 'Wow, I should make memories of this for her to read and look at,' I thought while the third batch of babygro washing was spinning. I sat on the sofa with a lemon squash and a biscuit, on Amazon looking for the perfect memory book: I found it. One and a half years writing in it, a crazy baby boy arriving, a house move and a pandemic later, it's fair to say those books have severely taken the proverbial back seat.

Monty is almost three now and I still haven't put pen to paper beyond the first page.

I'm a disgrace.

*   *   *

I had the *YOU Magazine* photo shoot. Now, having put rose gold hair dye on my barnet to hide the preposterous attempt at highlighting my own hair and ending up with something painfully close to cherry pink, I had to do something quick smart. It said 'washes out in 6–8 washes' so there was only one thing for it: to spend the next two days washing my hair at least eight times. Because turns out they lied and six is not even close to enough – believe me, I counted the washes meticulously. Because I was wasting what seemed like half my life with my head over the bath while sustaining multiple neck injuries, my daughter perturbed that I had suddenly developed a unhealthy obsession with clean hair, asking worriedly mid-wash, 'I don't understand why me and Monty only have to wash our hair twice a week and you've washed yours four times today.'

The good news is though, at the photo shoot, my hair was *almost* where it was before I started this whole malarkey. I strutted my stuff, fluffing my straw-like, over-dyed, excessively washed locks, bringing unwanted attention to the one part of me I totally didn't need any focus on.

'Is that pink in your hair?'

I stopped in my tracks

'Um, no.'

'It looks great.'

'I mean, yes.'

And there it was: I actually loved the pink hair. What came to light after that ridiculous panic-stricken debacle is that, at 39 years old, you can in fact have whatever colour hair you want because, well, you're an adult.

Next came the interview. The thing about interviews is, well, I don't know, I've never been interviewed before. Well, I lie: I have once before – in Year 10, when myself and three friends did a video for drama class at my grandmother's house, pretending to be news reporters with a mic made out of the middle of a bog roll with foil screwed up on the end, but I'm not sure that counts. But because you can't really prepare for interviews, it's safe to say I was a tad nervous, that's all. That is all.

The journalist began by telling me that the editor of the *Mail on Sunday* and his wife like my stuff and follow me, that he wanted *YOU* to do a feature and it would be all about female TikTok comediennes. It has made me laugh a few times when people have asked when I'm going on tour and when will they be able to buy tickets for my stand-up. I'm sorry, WHAT?! Are you out of your mind? There's not a huge amount that scares me. In fact, I'm a bit of a thrill-seeker. And quite like to be scared. I've done bungee jumps and skydives and that really scary ride at Alton Towers. That last one definitely proves it. However, the idea of stand-up terrifies me. People are surprised by this, but maybe it's because my background and passion is acting. Stand-up is a sort of humorous version of public speaking, which I'm also not a fan of. There's a massive element of being yourself as a stand-up, even though you're still 'performing', but on the whole I write fabricated scripts or use other scripts, which I then act out comically. Oh, and I write books apparently. Non-fiction ones. As myself. With my humour. And my stories. Which definitely doesn't leave you open wide to opinions and criticism. Wait, um ...

Look ... Simply put, I will not be doing any stand-up in the future.

'CK' IS FOR 'FOR F*CK'S SAKE' ...

When publication day for my *YOU Magazine* interview came, I was on tenterhooks. 'This is going to be pretty special,' I thought. The interview was an hour long. I talked about how I was writing a comedy sitcom. How my passion was to be an actress. How I had just run 100 days for the NSPCC. I even gave them a link for those who fancied giving a cheeky donation. I couldn't wait to see it.

Sorry, what? NINE. SENTENCES. I mean, I'm no magazine editor but I think someone must be a bit trigger-happy in the editing suite. Nine sentences. From an hour-long interview? For f*ck's sake. I mustn't grumble, it's all exposure. Hang on ... They said I was 'self-deprecating with an acerbic wit'. Why, thank you. I'll take what I can get.

*   *   *

The director of the film, Chris, and I have become quite good friends since he got in touch. Probably because I don't have an agent as a 'go-between'. And by 'good friends', he'd probably say we had an hour-long video call where we had a similar sense of humour, got on quite well and then exchanged a few WhatsApp messages after. What I hear is the whole family will be invited to LA for Thanksgiving and should Adam and I ever renew our vows, he will be best man.

I haven't heard anything about the sodding film for a few weeks when a WhatsApp message comes through from Chris (have I mentioned his name yet? He's the director, you know), saying I should be hearing from the casting director soon. I immediately google her name. Oh, for f*ck's sake. She's only the person who's cast the last 13 Bond films. I mean, why did he feel I needed to know this information? I suppose if it hadn't been for my googling, I WOULDN'T have known this information, but still I'm curious. And I'm also someone who hasn't done an audition in 14 years so obviously will want to freak myself out by looking into every detail of what I'm about to do. Is that his fault? No. Am I going to blame him? Absolutely.

YES!!! I got the email. From someone with the same surname as the casting director and she *is* a casting director, just not the same one who I had been told about. They're obviously related and work together. If the acting thing doesn't work out, I can always go into detective work.

'Chris the director would like you to read for the part of Sophie.'

OK, that's cool. Let's have a look at the character synopsis. She's a WHAT? A 22-year-old intern? I mean, I've been told I have alright skin in the past, that I take after my mother, who also looks like my sister, and that I could pass for a 35-year-old, but I'm not quite sure passing as a 35-year-old is going to be enough to convince the audience I'm fresh out of uni.

I'm going to audition via a 'self-tape' at home. This is when you don't go to an actual live audition, but you set up your phone at home, with a blank background and record yourself saying the lines either to no one off camera, or someone who's a member of your family, who sits on a chair, doesn't engage with you, has their head in the script and talks in a really unhelpful monotone. Yeah, I need someone to read that part. I call up a mum from my daughter's school. Not just any mum through 'eeny meeny' on the WhatsApp group. That would be a little odd, particularly when calling in such a huge favour. I phone one of the few I call a good friend and ask her if she wouldn't mind popping over to read the lines of the other part off-camera. I mentioned her earlier. She has the daughter who is obsessed with pubs too. Yeah that one. She's just got a part in her village am-dram play of *A Midsummer Night's Dream*, so suddenly I'm very excited, because in my mind she has now trained at the Royal Shakespeare Company. There's a hint of 'I can definitely do this' about her voice and, besides, I know she would jump at helping me with pretty much anything. Her name is Laurie. I quickly let her know that Adam will be here to look after our four kids while we do the audition in the spare room at the top of the house. Now I'm saying this out loud, I don't think I've properly thought it through. I mean, our two are hard enough to cope with. Throw in another four-year-old and a just-turned two-year-old whose mummy has just disappeared in a random house and there's only one way this is going to go.

Undeterred, Laurie arrives. We head upstairs – we have an hour to nail two scenes before Laurie has to get back home for her friend arriving. We get through half a page when I start struggling with my lines. She prompts me three times in a row, gives me an encouraging nod, I get stuck once more and then she caringly, with an undertone of frustration, asks me, 'So, um …' She clears her throat, 'Have you learnt the lines?'

In an ambiguous voice, I say, 'Well, yessss. Of course, I've LEARNT the lines. I just haven't refreshed my brain by looking at them after learning them. And that's very important. Look, give me five minutes to glance over them.'

Then, I hear Monty crying: 'Where's Mummy? I want to show Mummy something.' Seriously, how is it MY child who needs his mummy when his father is with him in his own house with all his toys and a bloody paddling pool? I hear him coming up the stairs.

'Ssshhh! I don't think he'll come all the way up here. Let me call Adam on my phone to get him.'

I felt a little harsh but, let's be honest, he probably just wanted to show me a Lego plane/car hybrid he had made and when I wasn't right next to him when he wanted to show this masterpiece, he was just p*ssed off. As much as I was extremely keen on whatever it was he was eager to show me, I'm not quite sure it was up there on a par with a possible life-changing opportunity that I had attempted 13 times and now had 42 minutes to get right.

I heard him reach the top floor. He was talking away happily to himself about, yes, indeed, his Lego. I opened the bedroom door to let him know Mummy was just doing some work and would be down soon to be greeted by a naked boy and a clump of chocolate ice cream he had dropped on the stairs. I touched it to double-check. No, not ice cream. I smelt it to triple-check. Did I need to? No, I had already touched it with my bare finger – which was also totally unnecessary and something I had never done before, and delayed things further, which was nice.

'Yep, that's toddler poo,' I said to Laurie.

For f*ck's sake. That said, it was an impressive-sized turd for a two-year-old. That is, unless Adam just hadn't quite made it to the loo on time, with all the distractions of looking after the kids. No, I'm kidding – he only doesn't make it to the loo and sh*ts on the stairs when England are playing.

LIFE LESSON
ACCORDING TO CLARA BATTEN: 6

**ANYTHING THAT LOOKS LIKE POO,
DON'T JUST ASSUME THAT IT IS POO.**

Double-check by putting your finger in it, smelling it
and maybe even tasting it. They are all very good
ideas that you'll never regret.

The next half an hour was tainted by numerous distractions. Laurie's boy, Max, went into meltdown after realising his mummy wasn't in fact in the children's ankle-high paddling pool with him, Cressy shouting upstairs, asking where her princess dresses were, and a sudden downpour of tropical-like rain on the skylight which, although soothing if you want white noise to go to sleep to, doesn't work particularly well on an audition tape where you want the people watching to stay awake and ultimately hear what the bloody hell you're saying.

I thanked Laurie and although we got a quarter of each scene done, with muffled screams and intermittent rain sounds, it wasn't quite going to work as an audition.

We went downstairs and gave the kids leftover spaghetti Bolognese and some token chopped cucumber, carrots and tomatoes for health purposes. (If in doubt, and you can't be arsed to cook, always have salad and raw veg to hand.) Then we whacked some stuff on the barbecue in case the spag Bol wasn't up to their standards. Cressy and Bella refused to take off their princess dresses to eat or even to paddle in the paddling pool, come to think of it. Now, if there's ever a dish I would like the kids to have while in their princess or party dresses (which, incidentally, I'm never quite sure if I have to dry clean, handwash or wash on cool), it's got to be spaghetti Bolognese. Yep, and there it is ... splatters of reddish-orange, oily, meaty tomato sauce all over both of their beautiful dresses. This leads me onto ...

LIFE LESSON
ACCORDING TO CLARA BATTEN: 7

Kids aged approximately four or five must only wear party dresses in either rain, –2 degrees, supermarkets or when spaghetti Bolognese is being served. Wearing them to actual birthday parties is completely unacceptable and unreasonable.

It's a Saturday, and I need to have this audition with the casting director by Monday morning. Right, Plan B.

As if I have a Plan B.

I need someone with zero kids in tow. Someone who won't let me down when I 'book them' to come on Sunday after a Saturday night out. I know, I'll call the biggest p*ss-head I know. Someone who has no responsibilities, loves a night out and may or may not have sent me drunken videos regularly of her on the lash at 2 a.m. I bring to you Sophia. There's a method to my madness: she's local and … well, she's local. No, it's more that she has no kids and, although she is all of the above, she genuinely wouldn't let a friend down and will be there to help, no matter what. I leave her a voice note on WhatsApp at 7 p.m. It didn't surprise me that her voice note back came with a lot of background noise, clinking of glasses, raised voices, laughter and a 'Yes, mate, I'll have another large glass of white'. Absolutely no jealousy here. I get to do stuff like that all the time. How I long for a night in, but not a normal night in, watching a movie with a glass of wine. I mean, one like clearing up playdough and slime off the carpet and battling with some kids over putting pyjamas on. That's what I really crave.

No, I can't complain too much. I have great Saturday nights. I pour a glass of wine or a G&T at 5 p.m. while I cook the kids supper. Five p.m. is night-time, right? I get to do this at 2 p.m. sometimes if we've had a BBQ. A BBQ means you can drink alcohol, whatever time it may be –

that's just a rule. I'm pretty sure it might actually be law. Sometimes I've started prepping the salads for a barbecue at 11 a.m. That counts too.

So, I let Sophia know what the scene involves. Me coming into shot and giving her a glass of wine. As luck would have it, I had a bottle chilling in the fridge as we spoke. I just happened to mention this, off the cuff, not for any ammunition. Now I'm not calling her an alcoholic by any stretch but I'm pretty certain this sealed the deal, and with an 'I'm there' she was booked for a script reading session at midday the following day.

Sophia arrives bang on time. Adam takes the kids out. Already, things are looking great. Like, 1,000 per cent better than yesterday – I'm easily pleased. And now the whole thing is going very well indeed. I do notice that because I'm self-taping and not at an actual audition, it's much easier to do it again and again. But equally bloody annoying as it gives you the chance to analyse the slightest movement or delivery of a line. I continue to do more and more takes. I'm not drinking my glass of wine as I'm talking, I'm acting. More importantly, I'm auditioning. I'm being as close to a pro as I can get, which is still pretty far off.

Sophia, however, is very relaxed, sitting back in her chair off-camera. Script in one hand, glass of wine in the other and me topping it up for each new take to make it look like I've just come back from a bar with a full glass for her. She's very complimentary of my acting and delivery of all the lines. Which might mean something if she hadn't already had the best part of half a bottle of wine in 30 minutes, or if I could guarantee everyone at the cinema would have just necked two large glasses of wine before sitting down. She's actually doing a bloody good job though, all drinking considered, and I can't pretend I wouldn't be doing the same thing if the roles were reversed. After both looking through numerous takes of the two scenes, we decide on the best of each.

We're done. That's it, it's actually done. Sent. Holy sh*t. I drain the rest of the wine – the two sips that are left, anyway – in celebration.

*   *   *

As I don't have an agent, I have heard back personally from the director. He's only bloody gone and given me the best feedback I could ever wish for: 'The writers, producers and I thought you were excellent.'

Oh. My. God.

He goes on, 'But sadly, not for the part of Sophie. We need her to be young.'

No sh*t, Sherlock.

Now, I know I'm not the only one who feels like this, but the only way I know I'm not young, genuinely, is because there's a number which tells me how long I've been on this earth. And the fact I can't go on really big nights out anymore. Oh, and that I turn the music down in the car so I can concentrate on what I'm looking out for. And that I drink gin and tonics and not Archers and lemonade. OK, so it turns out there are quite a few things which signify that I Am. Getting. Older.

But really, it's odd. I've always heard 'older people' say, 'I'm 51 but I don't feel it' and always thought, 'OK, you're trying to sound a bit "cool" now.' But only now that I'm older do I know what the hell they were banging on about. I'm genuinely shocked when people call me middle-aged or when kids take the p*ss out of 'Mum TikTok' when the algorithm gets it wrong and they disappointingly happen across one of my videos. I still feel young, I'm light-hearted, have a relaxed, laid-back attitude and I don't take myself seriously. Yet I know that 40 is considered 'not that young', even though in my twenties I used to feel bloody pleased with myself when quoting '1981' as my birth year. People would say, 'Gosh, you were born in the eighties, you're so young.' Now they react with, 'Bloody hell, early eighties ... getting on a bit.'

What a lot of young people don't get though (patronising much) is that you categorically get 'cooler' into your middle age. WHAT?! You DO! Bear with me. Not how teenagers define cool. Not in a trendy outfit way, in popularity, being able to dance, the ability to make friends easily, or by being 'Instagram worthy'. Not in those ways. I mean, in the more worldly, more secure in oneself and therefore more self-deprecating, quicker-witted, knowing not to give a sh*t and when to filter out the rubbish kind of way.

For example, when my friend Philly and I came back to writing a comedy series that we started 10 years ago (more on which later, you lucky things), we both laughed (and cringed) at the immaturity of what we found funny or what we thought worked back then. And at 29 years old, we wrote that. Not young. Well into adulthood. It just shows that age really is a number and albeit my joke mum dances and self-deprecating wife sketches, there are ways you are far more 'cooler' in your older years than even in your late twenties.

ANYWAY, the director let me know they only had a few parts left, which were mainly male roles, but he was putting me forward for the roles of Stuart and Gary. I mean, I think I'm an alright actor and I'm extremely dedicated, but I'm not sure I can change gender just for this role.

And yet! I'm reminded of writing this sitcom with Philly. Every so often I would read all the lines of different parts we had written and every time I read the part of Jeremy, the main protagonist, she would say I had him spot-on, exactly how she imagined him when she first thought up this character – the voice, the mannerisms. She kept saying that I would have to play him. It was a running joke at the start but as the years went on I realised she meant it more and more. She kept saying, 'But why not? You have him bang-on. Nothing some prosthetics, costumes and a haircut can't sort out.'

And because I have had in my head the fact that I could possibly play Jeremy in mine and Philly's script, I assume the director of the film was thinking the same with regards to playing Stuart or Gary. So off I went on a big spiel about how I could definitely do it, how I could play any part, how my co-writer of the sitcom desperately wants me to play the lead bloke ... I was really going to town. He wasn't saying a lot in return, more a gentle noise of slight agreement.

'OK, cool. Well, that's all great. But I was purely going to change the name and character to a female role.'

Well, he could have at least interrupted me during my barrage of unjustified self-promotion. I mean, to be fair, it's not like we were going to be making ground-breaking history, even if he had kept it as a male role. It's been done before and I was only going to have about eight lines in the whole film either way. Yeah, change him to her – probably easier that way.

'OK, I'll wait to hear from you. But just remember, if the writers don't want to change the gender, I can definitely play Stuart or Gary. You know, the bloke roles.'

'Yep, alright. Thanks.'

I think I've convinced him.

'E' IS FOR 'ESSENTIALS' ...

I recently had a 'pre-op' phone call with a doctor. Don't worry, the op is minor. What, you weren't worried?! Anyway, I might tell you what it is for after I've had a few drinks. Not before.

They had to ask me some pretty standard questions that doctors have to ask even though they know that 80 per cent of the answers may not be true. One of them is, do you drink alcohol and, if so, how much? Apart from teetotallers, there's not a single human who has ever told the truth in answer to this.

I proceeded to say, 'In drinks or units?' to bide me more time.

'Units,' she said.

I said, 'Well, I'm so sorry, I don't know what it is in units.'

'So, why did you ...? Never mind. OK, in drinks.'

'Well, I have maybe two drinks a night. Like a gin and tonic, or a rum and coke, or a vodka cranberry – I mean, not all of those drinks. That would be really unnecessary. I also have a shot measure, so I don't just free pour, and have quite a lot of tonic or, you know, whatever mixer I'm having, and I try to have two to three days a week of absolutely nothing.' (I had read somewhere that they like this. This is what 'they' recommend.) I could hear her doing the calculations, but I was quietly confident I wasn't about to be reprimanded. I mean, I had given the quantities of what a Gen Z 18-year-old, skinny latte-ordering, fitness fanatic would give. Not a middle-aged mum of two kids under five going out of her tiny mind.

'OK, so I think you know that this is too much and you should try to bring that down,' she said in her best teacher's voice.

Wait, WHAT?!

*   *   *

OK, I've had a few drinks. The op is, I'm getting a polyp removed from my anus. There ...

Now, I'd like to say I'm getting it removed because it's necessary or uncomfortable but it's not. I can't even say it's for aesthetic reasons because that would be bloody weird and my husband and I don't have that kind of relationship. But it has definitely got bigger over the years and it's just a bit annoying that it's essentially a massive skin tag which 'shouldn't' really be there and serves absolutely no purpose.

Well, look at that, it's the next day, and it seems I'm absolutely fine to talk about it more and more with zero alcohol in my system. Aren't you lucky?

'Just be yourself in the book,' they said. 'It will be fun,' they said.

Right, I'm off to get a burger cooked for me by someone wearing a cap with an emblem on it.

*   *   *

Moving day for Mummy. What a joy! There is so much bloody stuff here which hasn't been packed, by packers we paid to pack. Well, 'we' didn't collectively pay for a thing, my mum did, but as I've helped a couple of hours here and there for a few weeks, I feel personally attacked. Anyway, after a whole day of packing up three more car loads (with the seats down!), the new owners arriving, waiting patiently in the driveway for us to get the hell out of the house they now legally own and getting a last-minute Del Boy stereotype to come and take anything we were willing to throw out off our hands and even give us a bit of money for it, Mummy was out of there. Actually, Del Boy was too polite a way to describe this person, because as my brother, Ben, quite rightly pointed out, 'Del Boy was funny, had some sort of charisma and actually became a meawlion-naire.' This guy had neither of the first two qualities and stood little chance of the third with the broken picture frames he took – some random, let's call it tapestry – and two once expensive but worn-out sofas which may or may not have been p*ssed and puked on by my two kids.

My mother has moved into my Uncle Clive's house as her purchase fell through a few weeks ago and although they are only a year apart and have always got on well, it's not the most ideal situation, moving in with a sibling in your sixties when you both usually live alone and you've forgotten how to give wedgies and Chinese burns. Clive is awesome, though. He has been more like a friend than an uncle or a father figure to us kids over the years. He's very funny and he's chilled and laid-back (apart from the very teeny-tiny Gemini traits that occasionally come out) and Mummy is also laid-back, was seen as the 'cool mum' at school and most of all IS a mother figure. A mother figure to a lot of people and I know will help around Clive's house and probably buy a few things like loo-roll holders (she may have already had her eye on that). Basically, they'll be fine. He actually moved into hers after he moved out of London while he found somewhere to buy so they've both been in the same boat.

Mum said she's looking forward to listening to old records, having a whisky and chatting late into the night as that's what they did when they were 19 and obviously they haven't changed too much in 50 years. So far though, they have eaten COOK frozen meals (yes, those upmarket, oven versions of less posh microwave meals), gone for walks on the beach with the dogs, had some of my uncle's weird and wonderful university-style suppers and a Friday night Chinese takeaway; he's watching a lot of sport and she's enjoying some historic documentaries and true crime on YouTube, in bed by 9 p.m. with a glass of milk. So basically, just as she imagined it. Such a surprise.

*   *   *

Today I was going to do some housework and/or 'work' then spend some quality time with the kids. Housework: right, literally anything. Even if I just throw out the dead flowers still sitting in the vase from Valentine's Day. Even if it's chucking some paper towels on the floor where my toddler has just dribbled yoghurt, resting my foot on the top of it and swiping it left and right. This all while pouring a glass of wine and setting up my tripod; a wig, some jelly and a policewoman's hat on the sofa at the ready for the next TikTok video.

'Can I be in this one, Mummy?' says Cressy.

See, quality time.

To be perfectly honest, one of the things I miss about the many lockdowns is family time. When else in life are you forced to stop work, spend every day at your home with family and only go out for exercise or essentials? In fact, and forgive me for getting earnest here, but we thought the 'essentials' were the food and medicine (and yes, they are pretty good for sort of staying alive and stuff), but the real essentials ended up being the little things we did together which we wouldn't normally get to do in the rush of day-to-day life. If only we hadn't needed to have so much trauma and loss in order to learn these lessons. During the pandemic, I used to do little videos of me asking Cressy simple questions about life and what she thought of various things. We went outside in the garden with a list of things that showed spring was here and we had to go and find them. Mainly because the school sent us these on email to keep the kids busy, not because I had the foresight to create such tasks myself. We made up dances. We made cupcakes. We went on a family walk every single day to the bluebell woods.

Nah, who am I kidding? I mean, don't get me wrong, we did all those things, but it wasn't all unicorns and rainbows. It was more we went outside to spot signs of spring and Monty went speeding down a big hill on his balance bike and fell off into a sea of stinging nettles. Cressy and I made up dances, but this wasn't without mega tantrums and stamping of the feet at getting the dance wrong. Cressy, however, was alright with getting the dances wrong. We definitely made cupcakes but they were those packets you buy where you add a tablespoon of water and there they are. No, I'm not THAT terrible. We mashed up some browny/yellow banana and spread that on top, along with some squirty cream and a jelly bean to top it all off. Sometimes if we felt really daring, we added some peanut butter. And we LOVED our walks in the bluebell woods, until I posted a photo of Cressy holding two that she had picked and Cressy asked what the comment had been immediately under it.

'Someone is threatening to call the police on us, darling.'

Good times indeed.

Spending so much time with my children back then did teach me another important lesson, though ...

LIFE LESSON
ACCORDING TO CLARA BATTEN: 8

OFFERING A PIECE OF BANANA OR A WHOLE BANANA WITH THE SKIN GENEROUSLY AND HELPFULLY PULLED DOWN FOR YOUR CHILD IS UNACCEPTABLE.

The skin must still be full-on the banana as if freshly picked so that the child may spend at least seven minutes attempting to peel it themselves to then ask you to 'start it off' for them.

'U' IS FOR 'UNWANTED GIFTS' ...

My father was 44 when he passed and every year on his birthday in June I imagine what we would be doing and what a happy, high-spirited grandpa he would be. He would be in his seventies now.

God, how I wish you were here, Daddy. To bounce your grandchildren on your lap. To take them climbing over rocks and jumping in puddles, watch them play sports as you did with us, cheer them on in matches, be here every Christmas, the time of year you loved so much, your beaming smile lighting up the room, your contagious laugh. You would have loved being a grandfather and you would have been such a very good one. It really hurts when I think about the 27 years you have missed out on and the memories we shared when I was young. The watching a movie on a drizzly day, the belting out of 4 Non Blondes' 'What's Up?' in the car, the takeaway curries on the sofa, watching crap game shows on a Saturday night. Sh*t, I miss those times.

I'm now almost at the age he was when he passed away. Well, a few years off, but I will be turning 40 in a couple of months. Just thinking of you, Daddy, being only four years older, has really hit home. I used to look up to you, in both senses of the word; this tall stature of a man, booming voice, big smile and definitely old. Why do parents seem so old when you're younger? Mummy would wear a twin set and pearls to a school play, music concert or sports day. You always wore a suit without fail. Actually, maybe I might want to start taking a tiny leaf out of your book and not always wear ripped jeans, holey jumpers and Converse trainers to school functions when I'm meeting the headmaster of my children's school. I reckon he thinks it means I'm down to earth. Most of the other mums are like this too though so it MUST be generational. No, but seriously, Daddy, if you think I need to smarten up a bit for 'school things', give me a sign. You know, flicker the lights or make a noise or something.

Waiting … Phew, you obviously think I should stick with the down-to-earth look. Guys, it's not my fault. Don't blame me. My dead father didn't flicker the lights. So that's that. Just as an FYI though, Daddy: if you actually CAN flicker lights, or move furniture around, you can therefore pick up a mop or use the bloody vacuum. Just saying …

*　　*　　*

My phone pings with a notification. One I had actually put in myself. 'Father's Day is coming up' – another day that reminds me of my darling Daddy. But that wasn't all. The note to myself continued, 'Got time to order and personalise if needed.' I mean, WTF?! I. Me. Myself. Had written this long-winded notification to let myself know, in a very detailed way, that I actually had time to personalise a gift for Father's Day, order it and get it sent to arrive well in time for said day. Bravo, me.

But did I f*ck? I was there, ready to. I WAS. Had I not read that notification while sitting in the queue of the Sainsbury's petrol station contemplating what sort of Haribo I should buy and whether I could pop to the Maccy D's next door to get some burger I didn't want as much as the other but felt better about, I would have been on NotOnTheHighStreet quicker than you could say 'Grand Big Mac'. But alas, it wasn't to be. It wasn't until I randomly saw a Father's Day ad pop up on my phone days later that I realised I had one day to figure something out. I'm not getting hot under the collar or anything, given I always tell my husband I only want a card from the kids, that we're trying to cut back on spending and there is actually nothing I want, so I normally get some red Lindor (which is actually EVERYTHING I want) and a personalised card. So, this is already way more than I had thought of. OK, who's sweating? I'm not. You are.

Me: 'Kids, today we're going to get on a train to Tunbridge Wells. Yay!'

Adam: 'Are you sure? I know you've got a lot to do. I was going to take the kids off your hands for a bit.'

Adam had a lot of work on, so I made out I was doing him a favour by telling him he could work in peace, on a weekend.

Me: 'Yes! You have a few hours to do some work in peace. I need to pick up some make-up anyway and I can get the kids a kebab while we're out.'

That sounds a bit weird, because it's not midnight and they're not 19, hammered, on a Saturday night. But they actually really like those grilled chicken skewer things with salad in a wrap.

We were on our way to the actual shops. I hadn't done this in a while. Not because of the pandemic, just because I'm lazy and buy pretty much everything online. But this was quite exciting. Particularly knowing I may or may not find anything that would pass as a half-decent Father's Day present that would match up to the chocolate bundles of joy in those red shiny wrappers. I was really living life on the edge.

I had promised the kids £5 each to spend on what they wanted in the toy store if we could do a bit of essential shopping for Daddy first. But something told me that would have worked better at the kids' magazine section near the supermarket checkout than an actual shop full of everything any kid would ever want. Most of which was significantly above the budget I had given them.

Luckily for me, we came across Clintons before we got anywhere near the toy store. It was full of Father's Day memorabilia in the door and windows and Cressy, being the sweet girl she is, proceeded to say, 'Mummy, we must stop here. Look, everything for Daddy.'

'OK. Maybe not EVERYTHING for Daddy. The shop's pretty big. And I don't have £8,000. I'll take it though.' I could already see a foil helium balloon for £1.50. Brownie points right there and for less than a Filet-O-Fish.

I quickly decide that anything they pick up that they say they would like to buy, I'm going to say, 'Yes, of course, no problem' to, because every gimmick in that shop is a welcome sight and far beyond anything I have managed to get for him so far. Because that is zero things. I've never been happier to see so many cheesy daddy 'souvenirs'. 'Daddy, You're the Best' socks? Go on then. The heart-shaped 'Best Daddy' helium balloon? Blow it up and we'll take two. An absurdly huge 'Amazing Dad' mug? You can never have too much caffeine. 'My Daddy' ashtray? Um, he doesn't smoke and that seems a bit of an odd thing for them to be positively promoting as a Father's Day gift. I mean, it's not the 1950s and we're also not in a Mayfair cigar shop. I'm going to get it anyway. Because I can. And it's cheap. In more ways than one. Unwanted gifts? Maybe, but it will look like I've spent a lot of time and effort securing these presents he didn't need.

'He can always put his cufflinks in there,' Cressy suggests. Ah, yes. Now I see, that's ACTUALLY what it's for. My four-year-old yet again is more mature than her 39-year-old mother. We left the shop with an A3 99p card (bargain) for Daddy, two bars of special edition 'I love you' Cadbury Dairy Milk and a load of other sh*te in a massive carrier bag, which the kids were sharing the duty of carrying. Even though Adam is allergic to cocoa, we obviously still had to get 2kg of the stuff, which Mummy and Nana may or may not be scoffing very soon. The highlight for me though was a pair of socks with mushrooms sewn into them, with the words 'I'm a Fun-gi' written along the bottom – sometimes I hate myself.

*   *   *

As with every other year, I had decided to give breakfast in bed to the Man of the Day. Which I was finding quite difficult, what with being asleep, in a very comfortable bed, at the top (aka the quietest part) of the house. In fairness to me, it was my turn for a lie-in. I always ask on a Friday which day of the weekend Adam wants his lie-in. He chose Saturday. Long, difficult week at work. It didn't cross our minds to think about whether there was a significant day coming up which specifically celebrates his role within our family.

So, when Sunday – Father's Day – arrived, I took my lie-in. Am I awful? He says not. But I feel guilty. Very guilty indeed, as I sprawl out on a memory foam mattress, under a feather down duvet, not even able to hear the dawn chorus from the birds outside. No, but I do, seriously. Or I would, if I wasn't in some sort of sleep coma until 9.30 a.m. when my alarm went off. So yes, apparently now we are parents, 9.30 a.m. is sufficient for a weekend lie-in. I remember when 9.30 a.m. was waking up after a heavy night and thinking I was just a little bit late for work. If I hurried, I could get there in 10 minutes, only to realise it was a Saturday and to go back to sleep until 1 p.m. And THAT would be a lie-in.

Anyway, what I really DO enjoy about my lie-ins is giving the hubby a little text from upstairs, letting him know I'm awake and that he can send the children up, relieve himself of parenting duties, relax and get in that hot shower – for four minutes – until the kids come back downstairs, asking if they can have crisps and play with slime.

You're welcome.

Whether I've had a tough week, whether the kids have slept well or bad, whether any of us have been ill, whether work has been difficult to maintain, whether anything ... what I absolutely adore more than anything is those two little people coming into me in the morning on a weekend, ready to say good morning in their cute little voices. Cressy always arrives with a squash with ice in hand (I don't drink hot drinks. I know, I'm a psychopath but I'd be even more of one if I let my four-year-old carry hot drinks up two flights of stairs so I didn't have to get out of bed). I pull them into bed. Hugs, chats, what will we do today? Doesn't matter, just them. Here. That's the best feeling in the world. And sometimes, even on my lie-in day, I wake up before my lie-in alarm just because I'm excited to see them. Today, I have 45 seconds of this loveliness and then Monty turns over, kneels on Cressy's hair (which makes her scream), farts in my face and whispers, 'Mummy, I need a poo.'

Brilliant.

Me: 'Adam, get back into bed, we need to do presents.'

Adam: 'Sorry, what?! I've been up two hours, had a shower and I'm in actual clothes.'

Me: 'I don't get your point. It's tradition – you stay in bed while we bring you breakfast and you open your presents.'

Adam: 'The key word here is STAY in bed. But I'm up for a second breakfast, thanks.'

We all hurriedly pull back the covers and push him into bed.

Adam: 'Can I take off my shoes at least?'

Cressy: 'Nope.'

Adam never needs expensive, glamorous things. He rather likes the more cheesy thoughtful things, which is great because that's all he was getting.

Adam: 'I love them all, thank you. But it's like you walked into, I dunno, Clintons and literally bought half the shop.'

Cressy: 'Oh my God, Daddy! We DID.'

Me: 'Omelette?'

*   *   *

Around lunchtime, we were approaching McDonald's on the A21 on the way to Hastings funfair. I mean, we weren't 'approaching it' per se. You can't even see it from the road and you'd definitely have to take a slight detour in order to get to that lengthy but worthwhile drive-thru queue. But I thought it only human, given the time of day, to ask my kids if they were hungry.

Cressy: 'No, I'm not. Not yet.'

Monty: 'No, I'm not hungry, Mummy.'

Me: 'Really? Are you sure? You only had some blueberries and an apple since breakfast.' (See, great mum.)

Cressy and Monty simultaneously: 'Yeah, we're sure.'

Me: 'Just quickly though. You don't fancy a fish burger from Old McDonald?' (Look, I was just trying to get on their level, OK?)

Cressy: 'Well, I could eat something. A fish burger or some chicken nuggets.'

Monty: 'A fish and chip burger, maybe. Um …'

Me: 'I mean, really quickly. Need an answer. Like, it's coming up. We're almost there.'

Cressy: 'I think I can wait.'

Me: 'I'll have to take your first answer. Adam, the kids are starving. Take the next right.'

Tangent alert: I don't know why I have an unhealthy obsession with McDonald's, both in the metaphorical and the actual eating sh*t sense. For five years, I literally lived a five-minute walk away from the 24-hour McDonald's on the Wandsworth roundabout in London. I would go past the drive-thru every time I came back from visiting my mum's, every time I came back from shopping or the cinema, and I can count on one hand the number of times I went there in four years of living around the corner. ALSO, given I had zero kids for three of those years, partied a lot more and could stop off for a good 'late night snack' and/or hangover cure at any time, that has perplexed me even more.

Anyway, I'm trying out an intermittent fasting thing at the moment and although it says you can 'eat normally' during the non-fasting times, I'm sure they don't mean scoffing your face with a 1,000-calorie burger and then devouring a bag of candy floss and two pots of £5 jelly sweets at a funfair, so I decided to be a little sensible. *Too* sensible, it turned out. I ordered a delicious, succulent, mouth-watering salad. A McDonald's salad. Oxymoron right there – or just moron. I always said I wouldn't be one of those people. Why have I done this to myself? What a ridiculously stupid thing to do. I sat and ate my salad while smelling and watching the whole family gobble burgers and chips. They weren't even the ones who wanted to come here. I'd screwed up royally on all accounts. I did, however, have a bite, the size of a gerbil's, of Monty's Filet-O-Fish once he'd had enough. Rubbish! As with so many other trips to this sodding place, I don't know why I do it to myself.

So, there we were at the funfair. What bothered me most about watching all of those incredible rides – the ones that go upside down, the ones where you can stand in a round circle strapped to the outside of a cage and be spun around and around so far in the air at weird angles that you didn't know where you are or what you're doing – is that I WANTED TO GO ON THEM. But we, the adults, the parents, were not able to do so because there were no other adults to stand with our kids while we were fulfilling our juvenile antics.

There was a part of me that thought, hey, our kids are pretty mature for their age and would be so enamoured by watching us on these scary rides, they wouldn't go anywhere. And they know not to walk off with strangers, so this would be an alright thing to do. That lasted all of three seconds before I slapped myself around the face and told myself to get a grip. We had paid £12 each for these wristbands for unlimited rides, so it's no shock to you, I'm sure, to learn that they had been on the bumper cars four times in total with Mummy and Daddy driving, having our own little (BIG) competitive thing going on between the grown-ups. It was weird, we almost completely forgot about the children's whiplash as we shoved each other up the arse, it was so much fun. No, I jest. There was no whiplash. Just a few bruises to the knees. Mine. Not theirs. My legs were too long for the massive thing between my legs. Not like that. Jesus!

Anyway, it was time to leave, we had a four-hour pass on our wristbands and we had taken many videos of them on every slow teacup ride, every soft play adventure and every crap train ride meant for two- to three-year-olds, and although it had been three hours, they didn't know any different and it was starting to get cold.

'Mummy, I don't want to leave,' Cressy said.

'We have to, darling. Our time is up.' It wasn't up, but what are kids not being able to tell the time for if it isn't getting out of watching them on another boringly slow caterpillar ride (who knew they went the speed of an actual caterpillar?) when it was an hour before bedtime? OK, two. But like I said, who can tell the time around here?

Cressy: 'Umm ... wait.'

We were out of the exit and almost in the car park.

Me: 'What?'

Cressy: 'One more go on the bumper cars.'

She knew what she was doing. The only thing she knew both of us would turn around for were oval-shaped shiny things which haven't been updated since 1984 and some-how stay linked to a caged ceiling by a J-shaped piece of metal not even hooked onto anything.

Daddy: 'What was that? OK. One. More. Ride.'

He was already ahead of us all, striding towards the dodgems, me hurriedly jogging behind him, trying to catch up, like an excited four-year-old.

Adam: 'Where are the kids?'

Me: 'Sh*t.'

QUOTES BY CRESSY

Me: 'Make sure you draw your picture on the outside of the card and write the words inside. Then when it gets put up on the table, people can see the beautiful drawing first and open it to read.'

Cressy: 'Why would I do that, Mummy? The words are much more important and meaningful, so I would like people to read the words first then see the pictures inside.'

Good point. I'll shut up.

You'll never believe it. I've only gone and got a bloody offer through on the film! A real-life acting role in a Christmas movie, my actual dream come true. Now, when someone says their dream, people might think fame and fortune. The big time. The Hollywood heights. Or the equivalent in their field. No. My dream, genuinely, is to be able to do a job where I'm excited to get up in the morning, where I'm loving every minute of it. And this, for me, has always been acting. Not sure I've mentioned that before. I had thrown in the towel on this before lockdown hit. Before kids even. Even before I was married. Then doing my little sketches online while at home, acting out comedy skits, properly doing little bits of acting, in sometimes 10- or 20-second videos, revitalised my passion for it. It made me think, 'Sod it, why bloody not?' Social media is the way the future is going and, in the worst-case scenario, I can earn money from video views (like, £14 at best) and sponsorship comedy ads (a little more), while looking after my two young kids and creating humour and laughter, which everyone needs. Who knew this was a thing? I didn't. Not for a 39-year-old mum. Really, I didn't. I thought you either had to have a massive YouTube channel, or be a 21-year-old ex-Love Islander. Eight lines in a proper film, but who's counting?

'R' IS FOR 'RETAIL THERAPY' ...

You'll be pleased to know that Adam had his first day film-ing on the movie I got a part in. Yes, you read that right: Adam has a walk-on part in the film. The director, Chris, has a bit of a man crush on him. No, on a serious note, he saw Adam in the online sketches that we both do occa-sionally and thinks he's rather good. Plus, the man crush thing.

Anyway, I'm not overly excited. You can tell by the way I'm not asking Adam what time he needs to leave, if he has all the clothing he's been asked to bring, if the trains are running early enough to get him there on time and if he needs a packed lunch, like it's his first day at school, casu-ally forgetting that film sets famously have trailers, hair and make-up, runners and ... erm ... food.

Adam tells me he has not yet heard back from the costume department as to what he needs to bring. Without a thought, and given it's 9 p.m. and I have the director as my main contact (and let's be honest, we have become close mates over the last couple of months, in my eyes anyway), I jump on WhatsApp to send him a text: 'So, Adam isn't sure what to take with him. I mean, I'm not sure what part he's playing but unless it involves chino trousers or chino shorts, a shirt and brogues/boat shoes and possibly a trilby hat, your costume department is going to have to provide him with something.'

I'm sure there can't be much going on in the director's head tonight, it being week three of filming, other than what an extra is going to wear the next day, so I assume I'll be getting a text back pretty imminently. I wait for ages staring at my phone while Adam works in his office.

'I can't believe he hasn't replied. You've got to go to bed soon.'

'I don't have to go to bed soon. It's 8.45 p.m. And by the way, it's been three minutes,' Adam replies.

Ten minutes later …

'He's read it. Thank God. OK, he's writing.'

'Cool, what did he say? Do I need to bring anything?'

I call back to Adam, 'He says, "Do I look like the f*cking wardrobe department? I'm trying to create a masterpiece here."'

Chris is not a dickhead. He's sarcastic but affable and, although we've never met, we hit it off straight away and this is the standard type of chat between us. Well, not just me, with most people apparently.

I let Adam know he'd better pack a couple of changes of clothes and advise he heads off to bed.

'Stop trying to get me to go to bed at 9 p.m. I'm not 12. I won't be able to sleep this early. I'll head up at 10 p.m. I have to be up at 3.30 a.m. That's almost six hours. I'll be fine.'

We wake up to both our phone alarms going off at 3.30 a.m. – you know, just in case. I go to hit snooze but Adam tells me he's up, he's jumping in the shower and to go back to sleep.

Oh, alright then.

The next thing I know, I've got a message from Chris (the director, that is) at 7 a.m. It's a photo of Adam in his summer chino shorts at the full English breakfast counter, with the tagline 'Better pins than I'd imagined'. And this is where the real-life bromance began.

Adam was texting me with updates. They went something like this …

'Had breakfast with Chris. Top man.'

'The costume girl Liv is bat-sh*t crazy. Brilliant, though. Real laugh. Told you I didn't need to bring anything. You might want me to bring *this* stuff home though – I look dapper as hell.'

'Just waiting around, chatting with the others. Quite a lot of hanging around. Wait. I'm on.'

A picture message comes through from Adam's phone. It's of Adam sitting in the director's chair pointing with an exaggerated teacher's face on him, with the tagline: 'I'm the director now. Do this. Speak like that.' For a moment I thought Monty had his phone.

I can't help smiling. He's in his element. It's so far removed from his normal tech job. On a film set, costume and all, sitting in the director's chair, talking like a five-year-old who's been allowed in the cockpit of an aeroplane.

I send: 'Chris is letting you sit at the monitor in his chair. Ledge.'

'Oh no. He didn't let me sit in his chair. I just had a go in it while he went and got the two of us some Cokes.'

Wait, what? The director fetched YOU a Coke?

*   *   *

I haven't heard from Adam in a while. Then I get a short video from Chris of Adam on set looking a bit clueless as to what he's meant to be doing (but indeed looking very dapper in his tank-top cricket jumper). The caption read 'Oscar worthy'.

Another message comes through from Chris, who doesn't have Adam's number: 'Tell Adam, if he wants to have lunch together, meet me in the rec room.'

Am I reading this right?

I'm actually finding myself saying 'Aw' like a proud mother hearing about her child's first day at school. They're sort of looking after each other and developing a bromance at the same time. Look, if that will get me another part in a film, Adam, you keep doing what you're doing … more if you need to.

It's been a successful day. Adam comes home high on life but trying to underplay it.

'I met your friend. Bloody nice guy. All the other extras wondered why I was hanging out with him so much. They said, "Oh, are you friends with him then?" I said, "No, he's my dad."'

Me: 'Adam, he's like, six years older than you.'

Adam: 'Yeah, I dunno ... I was in actor mode.'

*   *   *

At last, it's my turn. Luckily, I didn't have to get up at 3 a.m. because I'm only going for a 1 p.m. costume fitting before starting six days of filming the following day. En route, I get a call from one of the assistant directors, asking if it would be OK if I stayed overnight in a hotel, on them, as I have to be on set early tomorrow. Sorry, what was that? A night in a lovely hotel with no kids or husband? No thanks, I'm alright. What else was that? No cooking and no bedtime struggle, no nagging to put pyjamas on or to please get off the iPad, no trying every bribery method to convince them to do their teeth? And that's just Adam, the kids are actually alright.

They told me to ask the driver to take me to get whatever clothes and toiletries I needed and to keep the receipts. Needless to say, I was happy to oblige. The trouble is, our journey has taken us to a pocket of London which is bloody expensive and I genuinely don't want to take the p*ss. But unless we drive 20 minutes to Oxford Street (which would make me late), I don't have much choice. The driver stops on St John's Wood High Street. Everywhere

I turn, there are independent boutiques. I spot a tiny Boots and dash in to get some essential toiletries. An electric toothbrush and pink hair dye ARE essential. They actually are as they auditioned me and therefore have cast me with slightly pink hair and this one is a conditioner that literally washes out in two washes so unless I avoid the shower for the next two days, that's not going to work. The electric toothbrush ... Well, I'm not that much of a knob – I went for a £5 own brand one, not the £120 Braun.

OK, now for some clothing. I only really need two tops and two spare pairs of knickers then I should be able to pop back home for the weekend and stock up. The problem I have, though, is that every shop I walk past is a designer boutique. Now, some of you might say, 'Hey, you're not paying for it, go for it, live a little. It's a movie budget, why not?' And the answer is ... because I'm not an ill-mannered tw*t. Well, I'm not ill-mannered at least.

I can see the car with my driver in it, still parked on the busy main high street, definitely not in a parking bay, and almost certainly in a bus lane, stop or some other unquestionably illegal spot. I've been here almost 15 minutes already. I spot a shop which looks a little more 'down to earth' than some of the others. They have boho dresses and some cool understated jewellery. I'm sure I can find something in here. I go in and immediately head towards the rail of white and pale coloured shirts. They're very simple and can't be too excessive in price, surely? I turn over a price tag. £126?! Retail therapy for me usually means picking up clothes at Sainsbury's, Primark or on Amazon. To me, £126 for a shirt is like paying £32 for a McChicken sandwich. I cannot possibly justify that. Even the costume department on set are working to a tight budget. For a tenth of a second, I DID think of getting it and just donating it to the costume department afterwards so that I also didn't cause my driver to get a ticket, which would incidentally only be a third of this price.

'Hello, may I help you at all?'

'Um, no thank you. Just looking.'

Why the f*ck are the palms of my hands sweating? And how do I get out of this shop? I could just walk out now, normally. I mean I'm not OBLIGED to buy anything. I could just say thanks and walk out nonchalantly. But I've only looked at one rail. I've not even given the shop a chance in their eyes. And their eyes are definitely on me. Because there's no one else in the shop. There's only one thing for it: to pretend to be on the phone. I make out that my phone is on silent but buzzing, with probably the worst acting I've ever done in my life, huffing and puffing as I scramble through my bag. I attempt to make the buzzing noise through closed lips but I just sound like a constipated frog, so I clear my throat and roll my eyes at the shop assistant when I can't find it. I'm sure the sweating has migrated to my armpits now and my thighs. I take the phone out and pretend to answer it.

'Hello? Hi. Yep ... Oh no! You're kidding.' I raise my eyebrows at the assistant and nod my head towards the door, equally as overacted as before, as if she needs to understand that I will now be vacating the premises, and as I do, my phone ACTUALLY rings in my hand. I walk purposefully towards the door, pressing random buttons, blushing, looking straight down at my phone, accidentally disconnecting the person who genuinely called, not a glance up, and then pretend once again to be on the phone outside the shop until she looks away. As quick as humanly possible, I stride off down the road to get out of sight.

I start walking back to the car, pondering over the fact that none of what just happened needed to happen. Absolutely none of it. And I have my fingers crossed that the very funny and sweet guy in the car hasn't got a ticket because of the kn*bhead over here.

Hang on, what's that? Out of the corner of my eye, I see the sign: 'Shelter'. Shelter, you beauty! Even I know that this is a charity shop. This is music to my ... er ... eyes? OK, I'll run in there, grab something and be back at the car in a few minutes. I don't think I've been quite this excited in a long time. I look up again as I cross the road towards it and read 'Shelter Boutique'.

It's not like any charity shop I've ever been in. They have beautiful white tiled floors, spotlights, clothes rails organised by colour. Even the red rail goes from the darkest burgundy down to the palest pink. I mean, it's all gorgeous and quite impressive but I'm also ready not to fulfil the knickers part of this expedition given the secondhand element, boutique or not. I tentatively walk in.

'Excuse me, is this, um, a charity shop?'

'Yes, it is.'

Get in. (I've never said that in my life, but in my head it sounded cool.)

There are a few rails with the clothes hanging in groups of sizes to find them easier. I go straight to the size 14 rail. I grab two tops, check the price: £8 and £7, that'll do. I ask the person working there if there's anywhere to buy underwear around here. She points across the road and says, 'Actually, a few places.'

'But any places which have, like, packs of five cotton knickers in one? Preferably full brief, not lace and silk lingerie?' I try to explain, in an awkward jokey fashion, 'You see, I'm just up here working on a film and didn't expect to stay overnight and I'm hoping that during my 12 hours on set tomorrow, I'm not going to feel the need to show off my black diamanté thong and suspenders to the cast and crew in some sort of uncomfortable striptease purely because I've spent £89 for the pleasure of owning the set. Although, given the price tag, I wouldn't put it past me, haha ...'

Well, that was a rather awkward, one-way conversation which also did not need to happen. I congratulate them on having a lovely normal shop on a rather pretentious but beautiful street and run up the road to jump in the car.

I get in, panting.

'Are you OK? Did you get everything?'

'Pretty much. Apart from the knickers, but the nearest place is Oxford Street and I have my costume fitting in seven minutes. Don't worry. I'll sort it out, even if it means washing my current ones in the hotel sink with hand soap and using a hairdryer to dry them. If I can be arsed. I'm not that stinky anyway.'

Shut up, Ra!

I arrive at the costume fitting and the head of the department is a girl named Liv. Adam had already mentioned her: she's young, wacky, Australian, outgoing and, quite frankly, brilliant. I know we will be friends. You know when you meet those people. The ones you have banter with from the get-go. The ones who are warm and you don't have to try with. She has an unusual but cool style. In fact, all of the department does. There are netted tops, flowery flares, leather bracelets, green feathered cardigans and ripped boyfriend jeans. I feel a little plain and preppy, walking in wearing my Topshop skinny jeans, knee-high brown suede boots from Sainsbury's and a Crew Clothing women's rugby shirt (the latter bought for me by my mother, like I'm genuinely at prep school and not almost 40).

The part I'm playing is a sound engineer in a recording studio. It doesn't sound like much, I know. But let me remind you that the film is called *A Christmas Number One* and the entire plot is based on trying to make a song that gets to number one, at Christmas. I'm the sound engineer while they try to make this number-one hit – the sound engineer who used to be called Gary, but is now called Michaela. Back to the costumes … I'm excited because I love dressing up (not in THAT way) so I can't wait to try on whatever Liv has in store for me. I put on some dark purple corduroy trousers. Not as a costume, just because I liked the look of them and they were on the floor.

'They are actually yours,' says Liv, handing me a long-sleeved plain dark top with a T-shirt over the top, which would definitely give anyone who came across me 'Led Zeppelin fan vibes'. 'Try this on with it.' She finishes off the look with many, many metal bracelets and necklaces as well as some massive spikey earrings which look like you need a hole the size of a 1p piece to get them through. Luckily, they're clip-ons. I draw the line at mutilating my ears to that extent for a small role in a film.

This whole look is out there. And I bloody love it. The pièce de résistance is a pair of, well, I'm not sure quite what you can call them … They're shoes, but they're brown and oversized (even though they're my size), round but also square-toed, scuffed and tired-looking, with big brass-looking eyes for the laces, which are the thickest brown round laces I have ever seen akin to the size of my little finger. Basically, they're fifties school shoes for adults – equally epic as they are disgusting.

I say to Liv as I come out from behind the changing screen, 'F*ck me, these shoes! They're so bloody funny. What the hell?! Where do you even get something like these from? They're horrific but hilarious at the same time.'

'They're mine,' she said.

She could see that I wanted the ground to swallow me up but I still felt I needed to say something: 'Gosh, wow. Well, they're actually quite cool. They're really wacky, but that's wicked. You know, it's fun. You're definitely, you know, not going to see them on that many other people so they're really … unique. They're really growing on me actually.'

'Look, don't worry, I know they're gross but I love them as well. Confusing relationship I have with these shoes. The director can't stand them. He asks why I have to wear them so often. And now I'm making his cast wear them, even though they probably won't even be seen. It's just to annoy him, really.'

'Well, good on you and lucky me,' I say and give a thumbs up.

What?!

She talks about the type of make-up that the department might put on me to go with my character and what I'm wearing. If my top is anything to go by, it will be heavy gothic eyes and maybe a dark red or very pale lip but if my shoes are anything to go by, it will be zero make-up, maybe a bit of soot on my face and possibly a flat cap or beret.

I wonder what my second costume will be, whether I will be wearing the same shoes or something completely different. I mean, not that it matters. I'm just curious. I really don't care. I don't care at all, in fact. Not one bit. I almost hope I AM wearing those shoes so that Liv knows I am actually very fine with them. Costume two tried on; same trousers, black long-sleeved top and a Pink Floyd fan vibes purple and black T-shirt over the top. I'm exceedingly happy to find out that I will indeed be wearing those shoes once again. Along with the masses of jewellery I had with the first costume. The team take photos of what I'm wearing so they have a record of it for continuity and then I'm done for the day.

I'm heading out onto the streets of London to try to find some knickers when Adam calls. He's also in town after a job interview and, as neither of us have the kids, I tell him about my pant-hunting mission and suggest we go and have a drink together on the river, where we can sip a G&T without jumping up to peel a kid off the floor or apologise to the next table about the child hiding between their legs. It doesn't take much to twist his arm.

Arriving on the Strand, one of the biggest, busiest streets in town, I get excited by the fact I'll be able to pick up a multipack of knickers, grab some Itsu sushi and be at that boat pub we've arranged to meet at in less than 15 minutes. Turns out, there's not one blinking M&S or H&M on that bustling street. Lots of eateries, theatres and generic dress shops but where, oh where, can one buy normal bloody knickers?

I quickly decide that a cold G&T, child-free with my husband in our capital city, is way more important than not turning my knickers inside out for one day. I head to the boat, and because he's a true gent or perhaps just because he craved the drink without kids as much as I did, he has them ready and waiting. We bask in the sun on the open-top boat and put our phones down. We have a proper grown-up conversation about how excited I am to start acting in this film tomorrow and how one drink is the limit for that very reason. We talk about how his interview went, how he loves the company and can really see himself working there. About how this would really turn things around for us because, since he lost his business during lockdown, things have been tough financially and this would mean we wouldn't have to think about selling the house. Basically, it's exciting but daunting at the same time. If it happens, we should be alright but if it doesn't, we have a month for Adam to find a different job, or for my social media to suddenly explode and give me earnings of more than the £400 a month I currently earn, or for me to suddenly go from housewife with a single acting credit on my CV to landing the lead role in a film I beat Kate Winslet to in the next three weeks with no agent, before things go to sh*t. Because the agent part is the issue in that sentence.

I know that we'll always make things work and the love and health of our family and friends are ultimately the most important things, but this will really take the weight off. I hug and kiss Adam goodbye, tell him to tell the kids I love them and, with that, I head for the tube with a massive grin on my face in my soon-to-be day-old knickers.

*   *   *

After seven days' filming, being called 'b*llend' a number of times (an affectionate term used on set – at least, I took it that way), some bloody great sleep in a hotel, 5 a.m. wake-up calls, an isolation period in the hotel room after my wardrobe lady tested positive for Covid, great big giggles in the green room, some random dancing in the games room, a lot of 'Oh, OK, I'll have both things on the menu then', a death metal band playing in a church (just watch the film, you'll get it), fantastic friendships made and some very special brown shoes ... That. Is. A. Wrap.

What have I learnt from this experience? I know you didn't ask that question but I'm going to tell you anyway. It's not very profound so don't expect too much, but it is honest.

I have learnt first and foremost that acting is 100 per cent all I want to do as a job. And being a mother, obviously. Sorry. Mum first ... so long as gin or rum are occasionally present in the evenings. And by 'occasionally' I mean available most nights and by 'evenings' I mean from 4 p.m.

I also learnt how genuine and decent some people in the film industry are and just how many of them you can find in one place. I can now acknowledge that, without even realising it, I had sort of tarred a lot of the industry with the same brush from the many stories I had heard looking from the outside in but also from the brief jobs I had on sets some 15–20 years ago.

One more thing I learnt is how weird acting in a film is in comparison to stage and how long everything takes. It took seven days of filming for me to say my eight lines. Almost every line is shot and then everything set up for the same lines but a different shot. Then there are the reaction shots of the other actors. Often, I would be saying a line to a person who is standing in for the main actor. There was take after take and it was very 'in your face' at times. No, really, the cameras sometimes were only a metre away from your face.

It was an unusual process compared to the village pantomimes I'm used to doing – *they* take a different calibre of actor, I can tell you. On stage, you only get one shot at it, one chance to nail it in front of a cardboard set my four-year-old helped paint, feeding off the 32 people in the audience. There's nothing like it. Seriously though, not to sound like Judi Dench, but I guess that 'real acting', heart-pumping-in-the-wings feeling is why so many movie actors go back to the stage. But for them, probably more West End, not West Bromwich.

Having said that, making the movie was a fantastic experience. Don't get me wrong, while I'm trying to revive my acting career, I'll take anything – stage, screen, porn … I'm kidding! No way, I'm too old for that. But no matter how exciting performing live is, being involved in the movie-making process – the many months it takes, the professional cameras, the slick editing, the colour grading, the musical score running over the top – then watching it on the big screen in all its glory, seeing your own performance in the end result is an incredible feeling. And on 23 November, that, my friends, will be me … in about 2.6 minutes of screen time.

QUOTES BY CRESSY

Cressy: 'Mummy, why do grown-ups laugh more than children?'

Me: 'I'm not sure they do. What makes you say that?'

Cressy: 'Well, I laugh quite a lot, but nowhere near as much as you.'

'H' IS FOR 'HAMMERED' ...

The film's wrap party is upon us. The kids have been at two different summer camps this week and, coupled with me filming and spending longer than I ever have before away from them, along with a few 'Mummy, I love it when you're back' comments from my Monty, the 'mum guilt' is real.

I genuinely never really understood what this phrase meant or why people threw it around so readily, until I started being a 'sort of working mum' over the last couple of years. And I don't even consider myself a 'proper' working mum. I work from home, I'm mainly my own boss, I'm flexible, I pick them up from school most days and other days I just leave them there (joking, that's not usually necessary, thanks to Nana). I take breaks from creating content or writing the book to take them out in school holidays. I work a lot in the evenings when they've gone to bed. I only worked on the film for seven days and even then I had a weekend with them halfway through. But it hits home when they ask if I'll be here tomorrow, that really wrenches at your gut. I couldn't wait for a couple of nights in a hotel when I was filming. I was very, very fine with it … with not doing bath, story, teeth and bed. Fine with it until I didn't do it and then craved it. Simply put, one night is a lovely breather. Night 2, I miss the chaos and I miss the cuddles. Night 3, noticing every child walking by in the hotel while I tilt my head to one side and say 'aww'. But I think it's our right as mothers – sod it, humans – to miss what we don't have.

When I got back from the second stint of filming I wanted to give them my time. We ordered fish and chips. We chatted about their week. We watched a movie. I let them stay up later. It was the weekend and I was going to be 'cool mum' that evening. We had hot chocolate and sat under a blanket outside and lit the fire pit. It was bliss … Until Cressy took a toasted marshmallow out of the hot embers and put it directly onto her lip. The calm crackle of the firewood and giggles of the kids was quickly overridden by an agonising scream, followed by a mild panic of me swooping her up, forgetting the blanket was wrapped around us, tripping over, cutting my elbow on the flower urn I had tried to use for stability and hobbling towards the door of the kitchen in an attempt to salvage what was left of her lip, given the scream. It was quickly identified that her lip was, in fact, not falling off, nor did it look like something out of *A Nightmare on Elm Street*. It did, however, have a slightly darker pink look to it and after a cold compress, some aloe vera and three more cold compresses while we watched *The Gruffalo*, we were heading upstairs for some well-earned sleep.

Cressy insisted on a race. With me. Goody.

'Mummy, it's a race. You get the Calpol for my lip and I have to get into my pyjamas before you get to my room. Ready. Steady. Go!'

She was bombing up the stairs faster than I'd ever seen her, while I was wandering lackadaisically to the kitchen medical cupboard to give her a good chance of winning without it being obvious. The competitive side of me wanted to grab that purple bottle in three-tenths of a second, run up those stairs three at a time and be in her room before she had had a chance to try and negotiate taking her top off without touching her lip.

I had got near the top of the stairs and peered around the corner to see if she had finished. Her door was ajar but I couldn't see in. I heard her say 'yesss!' to herself in a loud whisper and, with that, I ran on the spot for the last few stairs, around the corner and into her room, overexaggerating my out-of-breathness.

'Mummyyyyyyy!!!! NOOOOOOO!!'

'What? What? You're in your pyjamas. You won. Well done, girly.'

'NO! I also wanted to have my teeth brushed before you got upstairs and now it's all ruined.'

FFS.

> ## LIFE LESSON
> ## ACCORDING TO CLARA BATTEN: 9
>
> When taking part in a race, always check before the
> finish line that the other contestant doesn't want to
> add in any more elements to the race, just in case
> you are not psychic.

The next morning, I felt really lucky. The kids woke up at 6.37 a.m. instead of their normal 6.30 a.m. because I let them stay up three hours past their bedtime. Result.

There was much 'mum guilt' last night. My daughter burning her lip, staying up late, the kids having less sleep and also wanting to beat my daughter in a childish race.

I just looked up the 'mum guilt' definition ...

One article says: 'Whether you've never heard of mom guilt or can't escape its relentless grip, it simply means that pervasive feeling of not doing enough as a parent, not doing things right, or making decisions that may "mess up" your kids in the long run.'

I mean, the last part is quite extreme. I'm not quite there yet, where I think I might permanently mess up my kids, but there's definitely some sort of work/mum life balance guilt thing going on. I think when you're at an age where your own mum was a mum in the eighties and nineties when it was pretty standard for a lot of mothers to be a housewife/full-time mum, you may often hear the words from that generation about how work should not be a priority and that nothing is more important than spending time with your children. I'm in full agreement that family must always come first but in order to put them first they will need to survive, by, like, eating and drinking and having a roof over their heads and stuff. Unfortunately, we all know that wages (mostly) aren't keeping up with the rise in the cost of living, so as well as the women who genuinely just want to work and further their careers, there are those who simply cannot afford not to work.

But, as I said earlier in this book, it doesn't always need to be that you must choose one thing and 'give up' the other. Because if we DID have to do that, we all know that almost every single mother (or father) out there would choose their children, which would mean no women would fulfil their professional dreams or earn and provide for their family. There would be fewer women helping the progression of science, or achieving medical breakthroughs, or being an inspirational teacher in our children's lives or being directors of finance businesses, or there'd be fewer women, you know, acting or singing in village pantomimes. There's nothing wrong with a mother (or indeed a father) wanting to feel fulfilled in their own right, outside of the home life, as well as doing the job of the selfless parent. Our children are at school most of their waking day anyhow, which means I can either stay at home with the washing, ironing and daytime TV or spend my time working at a job I am really keen on pursuing. Or I guess I could go watch a movie, play tennis and sip prosecco over lunch with another mum. Sh*t, hang on! Forget everything I just said.

My point is, it's about balance. We should be able to do both. And that's why we need to make it easier for mums (and stay-at-home dads) to work if they want to. Employers must give parents the flexibility to manage the odd pickup or drop-off so that they don't need to fork out thousands of pounds for wraparound care, after-school clubs, nannies picking them up and cooking dinner, therefore also hardly ever seeing their children. We need to give parents the OPTION to be able to choose to be a stay-at-home parent OR to work and still be able to go for prosecco-filled lunches and tennis lessons. Sorry, wait ... and be a parent, I mean. To be able to work and be a parent. I have such huge admiration for campaigners like 'Mother Pukka', who started the Flex Appeal campaign and ultimately succeeded in getting employees the right to request flexible working from day one. Boom! That said, the employer is still able to turn down the request so we still have a long way to go.

Right, where were we, seriously? Oh yes, the wrap party. I have to tell my children I'm off again. Hey, it's a party. They'll understand. They wouldn't miss a party. And when they get back from school, they DO understand. They even wave me goodbye at the front door as I walk off down the street to the station.

'Are you just making sure I've definitely gone?' I shout out to them.

'Yes, we are. BYE, MUMMY. See you tomorrow!'

'I love y ...' Their giggles dissipate as the front door slams. Turns out my guilt may be somewhat unwarranted at times.

My kids HAVE just reminded me though that, yes, I am supposed to be staying overnight as the party is 8 p.m. till 1 a.m. in Camden. But bloody north London? Whatever happened to central London? The clue is in the name: it's central, therefore better for everyone. But to get the last train I would have to leave 1.5 hours after getting there, which just isn't going to happen. Nothing would have properly got going by then. The reason I would have to leave that soon is because obviously I won't get there before 8.30 p.m. because no one arrives at a party at the time stated. I actually think that's manners, not rude. Unless it's a booked sit-down meal. If I've invited people to a drinks party, I'm almost p*ssed off if anyone shows up at that time. Mainly because, as the host, I'm rarely ready on time.

ANYWAY, I am on my way to the wrap party. It's in a pub and we don't have to be too 'dressy', thank God. Firstly, I don't have too many things in my wardrobe that are dressy, and, secondly, well, I don't have too many things that are dressy.

I arrive and, although I've spent all of seven days on this six-week shoot, there's a certain nervousness about turning up to a party where you literally know no one properly, including 'the host', which I'm presuming, in this case, is the producers?! I mean, I'm guessing, seeing as they paid for the film to be made.

I arrive at the venue and Rihanna is there, standing outside, raising her eyebrows and glancing at her watch. Wow, bigger budget than I thought and quite weird that an A-list singer is waiting for *me* before she can enter a party. I get closer and realise this is the girl who plays the part of the intern I originally auditioned for. Thank God they didn't adapt the part to be a woman in her late thirties – OK, forties – because then I wouldn't have met this amazing girl. She's in her twenties and is so cool, chilled out, young at heart and a young, humorous, spur-of-the-moment young lady. There you go ... We've gathered she's younger than me. *Just* ...

We walk in and ask the bar staff where the private party is and chat about whether we should get a drink in the public bar first. No, why would we do that? There are free drinks.

'There are free drinks, RIGHT?' Rihanna asks, deafening me at the same time.

'I would bloody hope so after the phenomenal acting we just pulled off in their film.'

So, we head on up the stairs to the wrap party room and help ourselves to the prosecco on tap. We both talk about how wine makes us really drunk, too drunk, ugly drunk, and that this is definitely the only one we're going to have. You know, a glass of free fizz to celebrate. We would be rude not to. Plus, it's the free drink on offer. Just the one then. How we were suddenly on our third is an absolute mystery to me.

Here we go again … Tangent time. I think these are actually my favourite parts of the book, to be honest. Hopefully you agree, otherwise … well, otherwise it's sh*t.

White wine, it's the devil. I am definitely not the only one who thinks this. Firstly, because it's bloody well true. And, secondly, because I've had so many people agree, but who just decided it was never a good idea to divulge this information to me. It took me until I was 32 to realise this. I have said it to many people since and the amount of people who concurred and said they had to stop drinking it is incredible. Even my sister-in-law, who doesn't drink much, her best friend, people I have worked with, friends of friends and, I was surprised to learn, even some very close friends of my own. Well, some best friends, they were. Now obviously it doesn't help if you're also having four or five large glasses of the stuff, but big drinkers or not, every one of them has said that white wine makes them loopy, gives them amnesia, makes them feel sick or, worse still, black out. Genuinely. They say they can have a couple or a few and then there's just that one which changes the whole course of what's going on and how they're feeling. Not to be dramatic, but I would even go so far as to say it feels like your drink has been spiked. Or at least how I THINK that would feel. No one has said it about red wine though. Oh, no ... But I guess that's not exactly what I would call a session drink.

My mother can't get her head around how a spirit can be 'better' than wine. How something at almost 40 per cent volume can be better with regards to the effect it has than wine at 11 per cent. Well, I'm no expert, but I'm guessing it has something to do with the fact that we drink a very small amount of the spirit with a much larger non-alcoholic mixer. If you look at a can of G&T from a shop, the alcohol percentage of the whole drink is 5 per cent. Those cans are pretty small too, so turn that into a longer drink at home or at the pub, the percentage alcohol per 100ml goes down even more. Even less than beer, which is considered pretty low alcohol, whereas a glass of wine is 175ml or 250ml of 11 per cent wine. But does that all make sense? I don't know – I'm going to have to read this back another day when I haven't polished off two glasses of the stuff.

OK, I've read it back and it does. No arguing.

So, if some best friends of yours who are there sipping their gin and slimline tonic, not getting blackout drunk and losing weight while they're doing it, have not yet told you this top tip, I will.

> ### LIFE LESSON
> ### ACCORDING TO CLARA BATTEN: 10
>
> **DON'T DRINK WHITE WINE IF YOU WANT TO GET HOME, REMEMBER STUFF, NOT LOSE YOUR PHONE, PASS OUT IN A CAB OR P*SS YOURSELF.**
>
> Those last two were hypothetical, by the way.

Back to the wrap party … The room is filled with people we sort of know, people we don't know and people we recognise but aren't quite sure how. Ten minutes later, we are at the bar ordering G&Ts and rum and Diet Cokes and … not being given a bill. Well, the producers ARE legends. I mean, not that Rihanna and I base our friendships or opinions of someone's character on whether or not they are giving us free booze: we're not that fickle. OK, maybe slightly.

There's an emotional and funny speech given by Chris (that's right, he's the director). There's a reel of bloopers shown on a big screen projector. Anecdotes told, cries of laughter, touching goodbyes and some rather dubious snogging going on. This wasn't part of the 'touching goodbyes' thing. Or maybe it was. Who was it snogging? Well, it was very dark outside. Almost pitch-black, in fact. I wouldn't want to guess. I really would love to tell you, but I have absolutely no idea.

Quite a few of us (I'd like to say the hardcore lot, but all I'm really wanting is a bed at this stage) head back to Liv's flat. She has said I can stay in her spare room instead of booking a hotel.

'Only if you have my favourite shoes back at yours to put on for nostalgia's sake,' I reply, as if I was the one doing her a favour.

Being a wacky Australian chick, who has just worked on her first feature film, I expected maybe a flat share with a couple of other trendy Aussies in Shoreditch, Hackney, Earlsfield or even Earl's Court. I mean, I'm just throwing out a few stereotypes now, but what I wasn't expecting was to go into a hip (not to sound like I'm 72) apartment she owned and lived in on her own, in the centre of bustling Soho. Not that I was going to be appreciating it much. I mean, I'm a 39-year-old mum of two and, although I'm bloody cool and know how to party bloody hard, I'm totally ready to hit the sack at 10.30 p.m. And go to bed as well.

I wake up in the morning and wander into Liv's room, searching for my phone. This is the number-one priority for anyone ever. Wake up, and if your phone isn't next to your head or in your hand still because you've barely moved all night, there's a problem. I knew I was running low on battery after the many videos taken the night before so I had it in my head after the charger was missing from my handbag that I had plugged it in either at the pub or at Liv's. I know, just call me Sherlock Holmes … But really, in my mind, there is no way I had lost it.

We've all been there. Don't pretend you haven't. You remember running out of battery. You remember the charger in your handbag and you remember going on a mission to find somewhere to charge it. I was tired, yes, not p*ssed. Definitely not. I sometimes can't remember where I charged my phone in my own house in the middle of the day, sober. Add champagne and gin to that. But I KNEW I had plugged it in somewhere. I started looking in the room I stayed in. I even looked in the living room, which I knew I had spent all of three seconds in – I couldn't even find a plug socket in there for bottles of vodka, cans of beer, ashtrays and other memorabilia I don't need to go into. I head into Liv's bedroom and just get into bed with her … and her friend, whose bed I had unknowingly stolen.

We order burgers and bubble tea (whatever the f*ck that is?). We eat. We text Adam, from Liv's phone, and we drink bubble tea, which has zero bubbles in it. They inform me they must have run out of 'bubbles' as this is usually the best thing in the world apparently. Well, I'm furious. Even though I don't know what this stuff is, how can you pay such a premium for something in your tea which you don't even get sometimes? I ask if they got a discount because of the lack of 'bubbles' in the bubble tea I've never even heard of.

'No, it still tastes nice, but the bubbles DO make it.'

'What do you mean? It's effectively iced tea for £5.50! I'm not even sure how making this fizzy would warrant the high price tag, or actually if carbonated cold tea would be something I would like to drink, but each to their own.'

'No! The bubbles aren't fizz. They are chewy tapioca balls, or grass jelly, or aloe vera.'

'Are you high? We could get something else to eat?'

These are turning into very hungover chats. I almost feel 19 again – but not really. As when I was 19, I never really felt hungover. Why is that? I've never understood it. It makes so much more sense that you would get BETTER with age at coping with the after-effects of drinking alcohol. You're more hardened to it. Your body is used to it. Your body is more mature. Your organs are fully developed. You often drink less when you're older, even on 'big nights out' as you may have children or general adult responsibilities. You've tried and tested copious remedies over time to reduce the hangover. So why the hell is not being able to cope with a heavy night once you hit middle age such a massive thing? Sod it, I think it started when I hit 30. Everyone says it happens to them, so that's something.

So, the bottom line is: Liv and I feel a tad worse than we probably should. We put it down to age but still go and get a hair of the dog, like we're 21. Everyone over the age of 30 pretty much agrees that the hangover struggles increase with the ageing process.

But seriously, where the HELL is my phone?! We decide to get up, get some fresh air and meet one of the editors of the movie just around the corner in Soho, of course. He orders a coffee and then quickly changes it to a Bloody Mary when he sees us ordering one each – 'Spicy, please. Better make my one a Virgin though. I'm still working.'

We call him a swot as we all clink our glasses. And we feel so good after that spicy gem of a cocktail that we order another, as Jay trots back to the office to edit our lovely Christmas film in the middle of summer.

I have to get on this next train. It's almost 3 p.m. but we've been talking at a random Welsh couple sitting at the next table, who are in London on their honeymoon (probably just trying to enjoy a lovely, quiet drink in the sunshine). But we quickly put a stop to that with our anecdotes of filmmaking, acting, costume design and wrap parties. I get back from the loo to find Liv talking about my social media sketches, scrolling through her phone trying to find some, simultaneously slurping her Bloody Mary. I bid her goodbye, congratulate the couple and b*gger off through Leicester Square, hearing a faint Liv saying, 'Oh, I don't follow her! That's why I can't find her.'

Wonderful.

*   *   *

I never did find my phone. Well, I say 'never' ... I didn't before I cancelled it, claimed its loss on insurance and used some sh*tty old iPhone as a temporary one, which had a battery life akin to my children's walkie talkies they never switch off. THEN, Liv finally mustered up the courage to tackle her living room, which we probably all should have helped tidy up. And by 'all', I mean the two of us who were still there in the morning, one of whom was still feeling so terrible she couldn't get out of bed, the other of whom had permission not to tidy up as she was out with the owner of the apartment, enjoying sunny Dean Street cocktails.

Adam gets a text saying, 'I found Clara's phone plugged in behind the sofa, below a load of crap.' I cancel the insurance claim and, after a load of hell getting the phone back to the insurance company, I realise I'm due for an upgrade anyway.

Brilliant.

*   *   *

I have a working phone and now it's time to sort out mine and Adam's joint 40th birthday party. I've just been paid a good amount (by my standards) from the film and I know me: if I don't keep a lid on it, I will end up spending way too much. I don't spend money on expensive clothes or handbags, I spend it on experiences, food, entertainment, entertaining, but I am still always looking for the deals. My friends would say I'm generous, that I don't mind buying the round in the pub if we're only there for one, that I'm fine with contributing an equal share of a meal out, even though I didn't drink … Nah, I'm kidding. That situation would never occur. But when it comes to saving on parties and big ticket items, I'm all over it. Simply put, I won't be stingy when it comes to friends and family, but I will be frugal when something costs a lot. Does that even make sense? Anyway, it tends to work. So, with this 40th, I will probably end up spending quite a lot on making it a big bash. A time to remember. But because I would have negotiated £21 off here, £32 there, I will be feeling quite happy with myself overall, as if I've actually SAVED money.

I know it doesn't really make sense, but Adam got the job he interviewed for, so spending a lot on a celebration feels right. Since he lost his business during lockdown, we've not been in the best position financially. It's been a little scary at times. But, now he's going to be a CTO! Nope, me neither. Apparently, it stands for Chief Technical Officer, which sounds pretty important but I still have no clue as to its meaning or what it entails. I think I may have asked four or five times what this new company does and after minutes of explanation each time I'm still no further along. I ended up saying, 'Look, Adam, talk to me like I'm a four-year-old. Just say in one sentence, very succinctly, what the bloody hell you and the company do.' I genuinely always feel like I'm in that scene from *Friends*, where they're doing that quiz to win Monica and Rachel's apartment and one of the questions is 'What is Chandler's job?' and everyone goes silent.

So yes, the last couple of years have been pretty bloody rubbish and for a long time we couldn't go out much, spend money on meals out, drinks at pubs, cinema, theatre, so the amount I would have saved there would have been a sh*t load if I actually went out that much BEFORE all the lockdowns. I've also been paid more than I have done in years, for seven days on a film, so I want it to be a bloody great birthday for the both of us.

Googles 'hay bales to hire for parties'.

*   *   *

By the end of the day, I have booked a local band who I've seen play at our local 'club'. I like to support local, small businesses and then stitch them up by negotiating money off. No, seriously, I know for a fact we are going to be asking them to play longer than I have booked them for so will pay them more on the day anyway. I've secured 25 hay bales for people to sit on. I've got a FREE marquee being lent to us by our friends Sarah and Neil, have probably bought way too many outdoor solar-powered lanterns and stake lights, booked the local butcher and his massive BBQ (not a euphemism) and ordered all the meat (again) and created a playlist of songs to be played after the band finishes. OK, maybe all this happened in about five days, not one, and we also have loads of playlists already on Spotify, but still I'm feeling accomplished and rather smug.

Gin and tonic, anyone?

'B' IS FOR 'BIRTHDAYS' ...

Contrary to proper adult parties, I don't think it's controversial to say that kids' parties are bloody boring and more than a little stressful. To my mind, the only way to get through them is to make them just as much of a party for the adults as for the kids. So, when Monty's birthday landed on a Saturday, I went to town. Seriously, I'm talking music (and not just CoComelon), BBQ, five different salads (yeah, this one's a good selling point), hot tub, prosecco and periodically stealing the zip wire off the kids.

I think I might be looking forward to this more than my soon-to-be three-year-old.

But the pièce de résistance is a mini-waterpark my mother has bought as a joint birthday present for both kids. Their birthdays aren't close, but it cost quite a lot, so there's no way Monty is getting this as just HIS present. Imagine what Cressy would expect on her birthday ... Probably a mini-ghost train and that's just not happening. Sh*t, that sounds pretty good though. No.

So, this thing is blown up. We start with the best intentions and promise ourselves that, at £300 at my mother's expense, it will not get leaves, twigs or that weird brown/green grime on it. We will take it into the garage after every day of use. For the weather might turn bad. The wind might blow it across the garden. Something, I don't know what, might puncture it. But it's freaking huge. It's heavy. Are we going to definitely take this in? I'd feel awful if we didn't. It's someone else's money we would be wasting and it's such an amazing investment, not just for this summer, this should last for years. Yes, we'll fold it up neatly after emptying the air and water out of it daily, just before the kids sweetly pack up all their garden toys, kindly clear away their buckets and spades from the sandpit without prompting, put their bikes to one side, turn out their Wendy house lights and then help me chop vegetables for supper while we sing nursery rhymes in harmony with each other. Are we going to put it in the garage? Are we f*ck! I mean, the fact that every sodding year in the past four we have bought some sort of new paddling pool should be testament enough to know this definitely won't happen, given it's four times the weight of anything we have previously had.

It's the day of Monty's party and day one of the water park. We're all giggling and joking with the other parents after a full feed and copious amounts of prosecco. We've got cake. The kids are going in and out of the water park while we attempt to put more sun cream on them in one-minute stints of them racing back to us to tell us how great the slide is and how Jamie is playing with his willy. We are taking family photos, doing mum and dad dancing on the terrace, chucking more stuff on the BBQ and at 7 p.m. the last people leave. There are no party bags, but Grandpa saves the day and, through his forward thinking, they all leave with an exciting dinosaur egg that needs to be put in water and looked after daily until it slowly hatches as the days go on. The kids got something too – they left with a bottle of blowing bubbles and a lollipop.

We sit down, the place in an absolute state – toys everywhere, damp swimming costumes on the floor, cake on their toy kitchen. Nonetheless, no bath tonight. They've ultimately had a bath. Anything that involves water is. Hot tub, a paddling pool, a hose, the sea, even a puddle means it's not necessary to have a bath. Water has touched their skin. Well, in any respect, I've heard bathing every night is bad for their young skin. VERY bad. Any skin, in fact. Dries it out. It's very important not to dry their skin out. VERY important.

We give Monty the option of 15 minutes on his iPad like his sister. And by giving him the option, I mean gearing him on.

He acquiesces. Adam says, 'Do you want Blippi for 10 minutes, Monty?' Now he's a funny one, isn't he? Or not. Depends where you sit. I normally sit on the sofa and find him a little annoying. I do find him strangely attractive though. Hear me out. Well, it's as simple as this. I looked up the man himself, behind his persona. He's easy on the eye, charismatic and also served in the United States Air Force. Fit. So, if you don't know who he is, he's an American children's entertainer and educator on YouTube. Real name Stevin W. John, his alias is this screechy, fun, brightly uniformed character called Blippi. Kids love him and, despite his slightly annoying tone, he is brilliant at educating kids in all sorts of things in a fun and captivating way, from history and dinosaur eggs to how our food gets from the point of growth to being on our tables. I notice he hasn't done any 'cows wandering around the fields to slaughter phase' videos as yet, but he's all over a fruit and veg farm and bloody loves a bakery visit. In short, he's worth $75 million and his monthly income is $2 million.

Tw*t.

I put Blippi on for him (and add to Stevin's income). He lies on the sofa and says softly, 'Today was so much fun, Mummy.' My eyes well up. I give him a kiss on his forehead. Two minutes into the dinosaur song and his eyes start to close.

Result.

*   *   *

The same evening, I have a WhatsApp video call with Philly, the friend I am writing the comedy TV series with. I say 'series' like we're knee-deep in the midst of writing our second while our first is being nominated for numerous BAFTAS. The fact is, we are 12 years into writing the first pilot episode, having started it in our twenties and writing scenes when we were in the pub observing the characters (namely the 'red trouser brigade') of Chelsea, Fulham and Barnes. We dipped in and out of it over time and now that between us we have accrued two marriages, six house moves, a couple of scriptwriting courses, some development in maturity and humour and four kids, we have decided to get our arses in gear and get it off the ground. Simply put, it is MEANT for TV. It has not yet been commissioned, but we have recently been introduced to a big cheese at a production company, so tonight we are fine-tuning the pilot ready to send it to industry experts and commissioners.

We are on the call, laptops in front of us, children in bed – let's do this. I start reading the script to us both in the different voices of the characters and, all of a sudden, her son is wide awake. She leaves him, but he's not ready for the Land of Nod. Not one bit. We continue for half an hour, attempting another few words before there is another call-out.

'Hang on, mate,' she says. Off she goes. Well, I may as well have a wee so there are no interruptions when she gets back.

'Sorry about that, he's settled. OK, where were we?'

'I NOT TIRED,' he says, rather loudly.

'We ARE going to do this,' she says to me.

Alright, Miss Tenacious.

Three minutes later, Philly is in his room, laptop on lap, phone in one hand, stroking the head of Milo with the other, intermittently singing songs to him while she has one ear on him and one ear on my very quiet, tenuously acted out dialogue. I guess this is our life now. Until we get serviced offices, where, incidentally, our BAFTA invitations will be sent to.

You might think it a little odd, sitting down to finish writing and re-editing a script after a manic party day. But when else would you possibly focus and get creative if it isn't after hosting 12 screaming kids, spending hours prepping food, running party games and drinking prosecco? In fairness, and all joking aside, creatively and comically speaking, a couple of drinks isn't the worst thing in the world. More than a few drinks though and you get into 'thinking you're funny but just being a little bit embarrassing' territory. We DID get it done though, three hours later.

'F' IS FOR 'FRIENDS' ...

To me, friends are almost as important as family. I'm very lucky to have a few friends who I collaborate with creatively, whether they're directing me or co-writing a 30-minute TV episode over the course of 12 years with me. I feel very fortunate to do these things with the people I love and genuinely want to spend time with. There are also the friends I've known for a zillion years, who, no matter how much time you spend apart, you are always exactly the same as you were when you last saw each other and that's something special.

A while ago, I had a phone call from my good friend Coxy, who I have known since I was three. 'Known' is probably a bit of an overstatement as, firstly, he was my brother's friend at prep school and, secondly, when I was two, I probably didn't know my arse from my elbow, let alone who my brother's friend was. Anyway, the phone call is what matters.

I remember exactly where I was when I got this call (as you so often do with memorable events). I was driving my kids along the road from an A21 roundabout junction towards Bells Yew Green near Tunbridge Wells to take them to Minor Mania soft play, wondering if a 40-minute detour in the opposite direction when halfway to our destination would be justified in order to seize a Big Mac and fries. It was a little unusual for him to call – we weren't in touch very often. It is one of those friendships that has been a lifetime. Where life takes over and you can dip in and out of each other's lives, but because you've known each other for so long you fall straight back into where you left off. There was a period when we would meet up in London almost weekly, when I worked 10 minutes from where he lived in Islington, just for a beer after work; particularly in the summer, outside on the cobbled streets in a very urban 'beer garden'. I would normally get a text either to see how I was, or to say, 'Hey, fancy a beer after work?' We'd spend an impromptu hour or two slipping back into old times, reminiscing and talking about his daughter and his crazy love life. I only had a couple of these myself, I swear. But those random meet-ups were great and I think about those days often now.

He called me on the way to soft play and he's one of those people who you never want to ignore. To him, I would always pick up. Which feels a bit odd as sometimes, weirdly, even with the best of friends, you might just feel a bit too busy, or get a 'I'd love to talk to them but I'll call them when I'm back' moment. (NB: Unless they call twice in quick succession, then you must always pick up. This is necessary.)

I picked up. 'Hi, Coxy, my darling.' I often answered the phone to him in this way. Thank God Adam isn't insecure.

He started by saying he had some news and it wasn't great but he was determined to beat it. Of course my first thought was the Big C, but then he went on to say that he had Motor Neurone Disease (MND). For those of you not familiar with MND, it's the disease Professor Stephen Hawking had and, although life expectancy is one to five years, he very fortunately lived a prolonged and successful life. It is a rare neurological condition that causes the degeneration of the motor system (the cells and nerves in the brain and spinal cord, which control the muscles in our bodies). This results in weakness and wasting of the muscles. But in recent years, and particularly the last year, there has been incredible progress in research and they are so close to finding a cure.

Coxy goes on to say how he's going to do anything to beat this, to help find a cure; that he'll travel the world for treatment – anything to overcome this. And he will. I tell him I am right behind him. That we all are. And with that, we finish the phone call. The kids are in the back of the car and they are very happy but Cressy 'hears' the silence.

Tears well up in my eyes.

'Mummy, are you OK? What happened?'

'Yes, sweetheart. I'm just a little sad because my friend is not very well. But he is very strong so he will be alright.'

'He will be, Mummy.'

We get to soft play and while the two of them bound into a mass of squishy primary colours riddled with germs, I get on my phone to do a bit of research. I look up MND, what causes it, what the treatment is and what the latest research has found. Significant breakthroughs. Ground-breaking research. They really are getting there. My sadness does a 180 to excitement and hope.

Immediately I look at how these are funded. There are many different charities and organisations which help fund the research of this disease and I suppose these are the ones who need the support.

I text Adam: 'I know what I would like to do for our next charity raiser.'

Within a few months, Coxy's speech has deteriorated significantly (although his razor-sharp wit is still very much there). It brings home how quickly this disease can take hold and how finding a cure, when scientists are so close, really is of the utmost importance.

I decide to do a 24-hour live stream on TikTok. Adam and I can't both do it as we have a three- and a four-year-old and well, we need to keep them alive by feeding them and generally looking after them and stuff. This one's on me.

It's the morning of the 24-hour live and I've had tips and tricks on how to stay up sent to me on email, texts and social media. I've had herbal remedies, natural boosters sent to me in the post, Pro Plus ordered on Amazon, Diet

Coke ready in almost 'drip form'. Everything, and I'm really grateful, but who says I'm going to stay up for the whole live stream? I'm certainly going to try as it will make more money, I'm certain of it, but I had a shocking night's sleep last night and I'm a little concerned to say the least. Therefore, I've continued to label it 'A 24-hour LIVE' and not, 'Clara staying up for 24 hours and streaming it,' like I've talked it over with a lawyer.

So, long story short as I obviously won't be talking you through all 24 hours of live streaming as that would be f*cking boring (and God knows, I even bored myself at times during that day-long escapade). I mean, it really was the dullest thing I've ever done. Really tedious. I'll explain with a few highlights. Or lowlights, as the case may be. In case some of you don't know what this is, social media live streaming is the simple art of reaching your audience on channels like Facebook, TikTok and Instagram in real time. The purpose of a social stream can be to promote a brand or service, engage a target audience or host a live conversation, but in my case it will be to walk or sit around aimlessly for 24 hours, being 'entertaining' for a mere 10 per cent of the time and probably being the catalyst for helping the audience fall asleep the other 90 per cent. Which ironically is the only thing I myself will want to do. You click a button on social media which usually says GO LIVE (I know, it's high-end, technical stuff) and then people are notified that you are live broadcasting. In my case, 'broadcasting' couldn't be further from the truth. It's more a 'chatting random sh*t to people and then losing loads of reception on a day out to the point where I have to leave my family to keep the live going and spend countless hours feeling knackered, freezing my arse off, walking around an adventure playground car park answering the odd question from a viewer, in between giving a running commentary on how many bars of reception I now have' type of a thing.

At this point I was four hours in and had 20 hours to go. That was when it hit home. It felt like it had already been a lifetime but I had really only just got started. It's odd. I felt like crying; I felt like coming off it, if only just for a few minutes. But I didn't want to let Coxy or the charity down. I mean, what I was going through was minor in comparison. That spurred me on. And no, it wasn't all bad – at one stage in the Live I had my PJs on, cooking my king prawn curry recipe, in my element; in my warm house suddenly feeling very grateful and it was definitely a highlight both for me and the audience, who I think could gauge I was happier in my kitchen doing something I love than walking around in the cold, separated from my family, talking to 12 people about how monotonous this all was. And at another point I had chucked on my fluffy slippers, a roaring fire was going, I had a rum and Diet Coke in my hand and was belting out songs on the karaoke machine to … wait … 460 people? Oh, God, but anything to keep us all up. And it's for charity. I remember saying to my friend Laurie, 'Thanks so much for coming over to support. I really appreciate you staying up so late with me. We're doing really well. You must be knackered.'

She responded, 'Clara, it's 9.15 p.m. I'm fine.'

It was going to be a long old night.

I made it to 4 a.m. with three other friends in my living room I had invited over to keep me company and then made it until just before 5 a.m. on my own but by then I had a horrific, debilitating headache. Everyone had gone to bed or gone home. I was on my own with little stimulation as I wasn't even reading any comments as I couldn't open my eyes. My head was throbbing, I could barely see. I remember talking to my dad up there, in my head saying, *Please help me get rid of this. I need to stay up and do this.* I'm not quite sure what I was expecting to happen. A sudden miracle? For me to just get up and feel fine again? But I was willing to try anything. I didn't want to fail and I was genuinely scared I would. I was drinking pints of water and swallowing a paracetamol and Pro Plus concoction (was this even a legal mixture?). Nothing was touching the sides. It's a closest thing I can imagine to what a migraine would feel like. Fricking sod's law, the one day I choose to do a 24-hour livestream, I have a rubbish night's sleep the night before and now a crippling headache three hours before I'm meant to finish. I was closing my eyes and pressing hard on various pressure points like I was some sort of trained acupuncturist.

The most amazing followers were here – they had stayed with me most of the day and night and they just started telling me to go to bed. I was so surprised. They kept reminding me that I never said I would stay up for 24 hours. They told me to keep the livestream going and just go to sleep to stop the headache. Encouraging and supportive, they were saying things like 'You've done really well. You're a mum. Don't make yourself ill.' And with those reassuring words I laid my phone down, faced upwards pointing at Cressy's unicorn helium balloon plastered to the ceiling and slowly closed my eyes ... And I don't remember another thing.

*   *   *

I wake, almost startled, like I should be out of bed right this minute. It felt like 1 p.m. I rush downstairs as I don't have my phone and ask what time it is: it's 10 a.m. Well, it's a good job I took advantage of that lie-in. I feel so refreshed after 20 HOURS of live streaming, having some alcohol, a heavy curry, belting out karaoke and going to sleep with a massive headache 4.5 hours previously. It will definitely be a movie-and-screen-time type of day for the kids. But I'm OK with that. I actually have absolutely no problem with screen time. My theory is the more someone, child or adult, is deprived of something or told 'no', the more they want it or want to do it. (The justgiving site is still there if you fancy helping the MND association research.)

I have never limited the usage of iPads or phones THAT much with my kids and although when it was a novelty at the beginning they were all over them and I had to say 'OK, let's go and do this' or 'That's enough', they quite quickly became disinterested in using them all the time. Now, I find it difficult to get them to sit down and have 10 minutes on it when I need to cook or can't keep my eyes on them. Particularly Monty. If he sees his iPad on the sofa (which isn't an iPad at all, but a generic tablet I scored for a bargain £20 on Facebook Marketplace), he just isn't that bothered. Because it's available to him, he just chooses which thing he would enjoy more at that time. And it's usually playing with monster trucks, trying to MAKE monster trucks out of playdough or Lego or creating assault courses for monster trucks out of bits of car tracks and food items. Basically, he likes monster trucks. My point being, my three-year-old who has never not had an iPad as the norm is just not bothered anymore and I TRY, my God, I TRY to get him on it (OK, I sound like Mother of the Year, I know), but when I need two minutes, when I need to get sh*t done in a 10-minute stint and I don't want to worry about him flushing half a loo roll down the toilet which has happened, maybe, you know, not that much, maybe five or six times. Put it this way, we have only had to call the plumber out twice and only once has it cost over £300. Winner. Or, if I don't want him squeezing the whole tube of toothpaste over the bathroom door, or tipping three large boxes of Lego over the living-room floor, where one undoubtedly escapes and ends up under my foot (which, all parents will know is the most excruciating pain one could possibly have), an iPad can be, you know, quite sodding helpful.

Cressy is similar, loves playing with stuff and doesn't see her iPad as an immediate go-to, but as well as the standard YouTube stuff she actually loves playing educational games and figuring out maths problems and reading and spelling. I have zero problem with that. God, I have zero problem with them watching Wendy playing with toys obviously gifted to them by their sponsors. To adults, this show is probably THE most grating thing to hear, but to children, it is music to their young little ears. If you know, you know. Adam, having a background in computers, has also raised the point that there is a lot to be said for children starting to navigate technology from a young age. An almost basic form of 'coding', how moving with the times can gear them up not only for a job in the tech industry but just the ability to use technology is nothing short of a modern life skill. Plus (and my kids, please don't read this part of the book as you get older), there are also teenage gamers and adult gamers who are actually earning millions in competitions, which I was so surprised to hear. But let's just stick to tech firms and 'coding' stuff for now. You get what I'm saying …

Adam says he can take the kids out to ride their bikes anyway as it's the weekend and I've been up all night, so that last 10 minutes of writing wasn't totally necessary, but I feel there may have been a few little subliminal life lessons in there which might be quite interesting to a few. *Might be.*

*   *   *

So, I've had another look and I have raised £1,600 in that 24-hour live stream, which of course is a great amount of money, but quite frankly, obviously nowhere near the £30k raised for the NSPCC and I'd rather do another '100 days of running' three times over than do another 24-hour live stream.

'Adam, I have an idea ...'

'NO.'

'L' IS FOR 'LOST TOYS' ...

I don't mean just any kids' toys, I mean the ones which they are REALLY attached to. They are normally soft, cuddly, sleepy, totty, blanky type things. Basically, anything with a 'y' on the end. They've normally had them from day dot and simply don't grow out of them. You can try and offer them fluffier, often more expensive, cuddlier toys – knowing they're from a big brand and made in abundance, meaning you'll be able to replace them at the drop of a hat – but they will still resort to loving this one thing. The thing most likely given to them when they were born, by someone you barely know, or someone you actually do know, but because the baby was given 9,263 soft, sleepy, huggable things the moment they were out of the womb, you have sod-all idea who they are from – and because of your exhaustion and preoccupation with a newborn, every-one is seemingly fine with this lack of knowledge or thanks.

I bring you YaYa, Cressy's 'thing'. It's a square piece of white soft material (Cressy calls this her 'dress') with pink spots on it, almost like it's had a bad case of chickenpox.

Or elephant pox, as this flat square quite literally has an elephant's head just stuck in the middle of it. The body is gone. Nothing. Just an elephant's head. I mean, this is enough to give me nightmares. But it doesn't stop there. There are random tags hanging off every corner and two off every side of the square. But these aren't normal toy tags. They seem to be embellished with some sort of psychedelic decoration. And there are 12 of the f*ckers. This person who created YaYa was definitely stoned when they dreamt her up, or at least drunk, but either way they did something right as my four-year-old is still utterly obsessed.

This thing comes with us everywhere we go. To say we have lost it a few times would be a massive lie. We have lost it (sorry, 'her') approximately 18 times and that's not including 'misplacing' her at nursery. And the fact that we have found her every time, I think, is pretty impressive. She's been left on an aeroplane, under a bench in a park overnight, in her drawer at nursery over the weekend after driving back at 6.30 p.m. on a Friday night to closed doors, at friends' houses, in an oven (where she was apparently being 'kept warm'), in a local pub (where, after we collected her, the staff said they had been dancing with her into the night after we left), in the glove box of Nana's car. And every time we eventually found her after retracing steps. But the most prominent time was when we left her at our local village bistro (yes, we have one of those. In fact, it's the only thing we have in our village, which is odd come to think of it, seeing as we can't buy milk anywhere). Anyway, this bistro has slightly 'unique' opening hours and when we went back at 7 p.m. on a Monday, the doors were locked.

Cressy was distraught. On a mission, I messaged a village group on Facebook with my predicament to see if anyone had the owner's number as they didn't live at the property. I had a quick response from someone giving the number and address of a husband-and-wife team I have since become rather close to. So, I called them to explain. I had only lived in the village for six months and they didn't know who the hell I was, but they were quick to say they would happily come back to open up and look. They very kindly did and after switching the lights on and all three of us looking inside and outside, behind the bar and underneath picnic tables outside, alas it wasn't there. Cressy was in pieces but three days later we found YaYa under the kids' chairs in the living room.

I never wanted any of us to go through that again: it was time to find a YaYa backup. We searched the internet for items which might resemble this 'thing'. I didn't know what it was called or how to begin the search so all I could do was type in a description of its appearance into Google. It was totally unsuccessful, but at least I could rest assured that if the police ever got hold of my laptop and took a look at my search history, I would most definitely be charged.

There were a lot of elephant toys. You know, ones with bodies. Authentic cuddly little proper animals which resemble actual elephants. But other than that, nothing. Absolutely nothing. So, we put a past photo on social media asking where we could buy something like this. We sent a message around to our whole friendship group to find out who might have sent it. Again, nothing. No one seemed to know where it came from or what you would call it. I attempted to do the same descriptive search online probably twice every six months, increasing my chances of arrest enormously, but being worth the risk to try to find a YaYa successor, should this happen again.

After a couple more years of losing her, finding her and not quite losing her again, eventually came the day we had all been dreading: YaYa was gone. We couldn't find her anywhere, even after retracing our steps. We suddenly realised a week later that Cressy may have had her on the morning of New Year's Day when she was being dropped off for lunch at the pub with us after being babysat by Nana the night before.

I quickly got the phone out and called said pub. They told me they had loads of toys in Lost Property – great – but that they throw them all out at the start of the New Year to make space for the next year's. I argue that technically this would have counted as their next haul of toys:

'Yes, but she lost it on New Year's Day. Day 1 of the year. In fact, this was probably the first one to arrive on your desk of a massive collection to come. So how lucky are you that you're able to find its owner within a week?'

'Yes. Very lucky.' I definitely detected a hint of sarcasm in her voice. 'It's just that it depends what time we threw them all out.'

'So, you're saying you would throw out a toy which has been with you a couple of hours, along with toys which have been with you for 300-odd days?' At this point I'm starting to question my part in this so-called 'grown-up' conversation.

'Well, we don't really think about it that deeply.'

'No, you don't think at all.' WHAT?! 'Look, I'm sorry. I'm just rather stressed about this.'

'Yes, I understand. I think …'

'So, erm, anyway, do you have any toys at all in Lost Property, as we speak?'

'No.'

Well, I could have got to that result quicker and with slightly less embarrassment.

YaYa is gone. Weirdly, I'm missing that little elephant head on chicken pox square. Right, it's time to search the internet again. I put in the same description as if Google would have magically changed its search results to exactly what I was looking for. I then google, 'what is the name of the toy children get attached to?' Search. One of the first results starts 'Your toddlers lovey attachment'. 'Lovey', hey? I type 'elephant head lovey with pink spots'. BOOM. The fifth image is YaYa. I properly weep. What the actual hell? I'm sitting in my car, crying my eyes out, over finding a £10 (plus postage & packaging) toy on eBay. And I'm sorry, if you're not crying now, you're dead inside ...

I think about sending a screenshot to Adam saying, 'Look who it is!' But no, I want to tell him in person. I know his face is going to be a picture. I mean, it's a tough, emotional ride we've all been on. And also, what the f*ck am I actually saying?

Sh*t, this day has just got better. The more I scroll and delve deeper, there are three of these gorgeous little spotty elephants from different sellers. No more. I've checked. Trust me, just three. But that will more than do. *Click. Click. Clickety click* ... I've purchased all three of the beauties.

I rush home and show Adam my phone.

'Look!'

He's at his desk working. He double takes then stands up in a flash: 'You've found her!' He looks almost as emotional as I was, in a sort of really deadpan way and without any tears.

'Well no, not really. Someone didn't find YaYa at The 8 Bells and decide trading her online would be a really good business decision but I have found another exact replica AND bought *three*.'

The first one arrives a few days later and we wrap her up, ready for when Cressy arrives home from school. We are a little bit concerned that she might still be quite upset that it's not the original and that the main reason she's upset is because YaYa is lost, not that she doesn't have a replica. She sits down, hands out, eyes closed. As she opens the parcel, she gets a glimpse of the pink spots and puts her hand in, excitedly murmuring, 'I know what it is … I know what it is … It's a new YaYa!' As she pulls that brighter-than-white square of delight out of the wrapping, she squeezes her so tightly as a little tear rolls down her cheek.

'I love her,' she whispers.

And if you're not crying now, seriously, get help: you're a robot.

QUOTES BY CRESSY

(With a special appearance from Adam)

Cressy: 'Mummy, I'm tucked up all warm in bed and YaYa is downstairs. Could you call Daddy and ask him to bring her up?'

I put my phone on speaker and call Adam from my phone (not because our house is big, I'm just bloody lazy!)

He answers, 'Good evening, 101 800 sex line, how may I help you?'

Cressy: 'Daddy, can you bring YaYa upstairs?'

Adam: 'Yes, of course, sweetheart. Gosh, that was weird.'

'J' IS FOR 'JARS OF PICKLED HERRING' ...

Yes, you read that right!

Adam's cousin Georgie and her amazing stepmum Barbara are staying for the weekend. I get excited when I see these two. Georgie is a good friend and Barbara is that warm 'second mum' type who is also just like a best mate you could tell anything to. I know that whatever we discuss, there'll be lots of giggles and zero judgement.

We got onto the subject of stinginess and how often it's the richest people who are 'stingy'. Some say that that's the reason they're rich but I don't think you can genuinely become rich by being stingy. You might be able to *save* quite a bit towards a holiday but it's not going to make you stinking rich if you're on a normal salary. We discussed what each of us would be like if we had a lot of money. I know what I'm like. When I was in my twenties I was actually making more in cold-calling media sales than in any other 'bigger job' I went on to have in real estate (OK, as an estate agent, but the Americanism always sounds more prolific) and I was definitely more frivolous with it. I liked to be generous with my friends, get the rounds in, or pay for the theatre or comedy night we were going to if they were a bit tight on cash and otherwise wouldn't be able to.

But as I've got older, and particularly since having kids and being more cash-poor myself, I'm more careful with what I've got. But seriously, we don't actually have cash at the end of the month after not really even doing much. Until now, I haven't worked since having kids and I have new priorities other than just paying rent at the end of the month as I did in London. Like little people I have created. You know, small things like that. Don't get me wrong, I'm incredibly grateful for what I've got. I'm much more fortunate than many others but stresses and monetary worries are all relative to a person's situation. I'm not moaning by any stretch. Many hear my 'voice' or see a quite-nice house on social media and think 'She's doing alright' or have said 'You're obviously minted' or 'So what sort of school do your children go to?' People are allowed to prioritise what's important to THEIR family. For us, it's our kids' school. It's a private school and it's incredible. We would rather shop differently, continue buying clothes from Sainsbury's and taking the maximum mortgage we can take, cut out some holidays, have one second-hand car, buy furniture second-hand or in the DFS sale and not have a handbag or shoe fetish (I keep telling Adam he has to cut down), even downsize our home if it came to it, to keep our kids in that school. And I know that won't be on everyone's wish-list, preferred way of living or be everyone's priority and that's also fine.

If I was a squillionaire, I would spend the money on experiences. Really nice experiences. ('Nice' is a good adjective, isn't it? So descriptive and passionate.) But I would and the reason why 'nice' is a very good word in this case is because it wouldn't necessarily be the really expensive experiences in life, not the finest of the finest (although I probably would end up doing my dream of chartering a superyacht with a bunch of friends and family). It would be mainly things like 'really nice' holidays (there's that gem again), but also going to Waitrose for every weekly shop and buying overpriced stuff which I don't ACTUALLY need to feed me or my family on, but which are delicious and I could nail as a snack but are totally overpriced for what they are. For example, and most people will not agree with me on this, but if you just give them a go, I SWEAR you will find them bloody delish. Waitrose do a jar of sweet pickled herring with dill.

Now I'm fully aware that I will not have sold you on that description but it's genuinely one of the nicest – nay, superb – things I have tasted. And that's not just under the cold fish umbrella, that's out of all foods ever. But it RRPs at about £3.50 and right now I'm just not prepared to spend that much on what is ultimately going to be a four-minute snack for just me, munching through the best part of a jar while stacking the dishwasher. Unless my mother is with us, that is, and gives me her card, saying, 'Get the kids something to eat for the ride home and also whatever you want.' In that situation, you'll see my car do a sharp detour away from Tesco and towards Waitrose. I'll run in quicker than a babysitter's boyfriend when the car pulls up. The kids always have a box of strawberries and a doughnut and I have a jar of cold, raw, pickled, sweet fish with some dill thrown in, coming in at a grand total of £7.25. B*stards.

QUOTES BY CRESSY

Cressy: 'Mummy, how many more words do you have to write in your book?'

Me: 'Maybe 5,000 or 10,000.'

Cressy: 'Well, which one is it? They are very different. I can help you if you like. I have lots of things to say. It can't be that hard. I think it would be rather easy just talking about life and us and being a bit funny. Can I help you?'

Me: 'Oh you are, Cress. More than you know.'

As you may have surmised from my Maccy D addiction, tales of day-old pants and habit of eating fish from a jar, I pride myself on being relatable. Maybe not the whole fish thing so much. Hey, don't knock it! But I love the fact that so many people message me saying they can see themselves in me; that I don't have the perfect house, that I talk and do sketches on loving to eat, not always looking great, needing a G&T occasionally, not being the perfect mum, on the trials of parenting or trying to keep up with the normal crap like washing or school sh*t, such as emails, and feeding my kids BelVita biscuits for breakfast when we're late. Wait, what?!

That's not always the case in the curated world of social media. The other day I saw someone on Facebook post a picture of their beautiful fireplace, no ash in sight. There were two family photos left and right of the mantelpiece, like stunning bookends with dried autumn flowers in the middle, and on a coffee table below sat a fan of glossy magazines. Caption: 'Autumn has arrived'. I wrote, 'Please tell me you tidy up your house before taking photos of these things.' Why has my mantelpiece got a half-burnt joss stick on it, like I'm 15 years old, three lighters (when no one smokes), a random battery and a Barbie shoe?

Perhaps that's why I have recently had two companies offer me their services in return for a little video or shout-out on social media. One has offered to do a full deep-clean of my oven, my hob and my extractor fan (yes, I may or may not have done a sketch taking numerous things out of my oven, where I tried unsuccessfully to cover up the state of it) and the second, a company called 'Bee Organised', which completely declutters your house and goes through all the toys and cupboards and figures out what goes where and if there are bits missing or just random parts of toys strewn about the place they get binned. Perfect. But I can't help noticing that her DM came straight after I posted a video where my beautiful antique sideboard is nowhere to be seen for piles of toys, playdough memorabilia and puzzles stacked up over the whole thing.

I take both of these companies up on their offers. After all, when the world and his wife descend on my house for our 40th party, I want them know that I am 100 per cent on top of my game and definitely not living in an episode of *A Life of Grime*.

QUOTES BY CRESSY

Cressy: 'Daddy's not even home from work yet and it already smells in here.'

Me: 'What do you mean?'

Cressy: 'Daddy's farts really smell but he's not even home from work – I don't understand it.'

'V' IS FOR 'VITAMINS' ...

Let's talk vitamins. Except it's not really talking, is it? Rather, this is me talking *at* you. The concept of a non-fiction book is a little odd when you think about it. I've read plenty and I bloody love them, but when you write one yourself, you feel a bit narcissistic. I'm a sociable person and love being around people. You know, having basic, good old two-way conversations. But writing this, albeit enjoyable, is far removed from the standard 'people person' I normally am. It's ultimately writing about your-self, your experiences, your thoughts on stuff, imagining everyone wants to hear it. Strange when you actually think about it. I've not taken any drugs, I promise. *You* may want to though, before reading this.

So, vitamins. Sexy, I know. Very sexy and interesting. You can send me a little DM with your thoughts on things in this book if you want. I'd love to hear them. I will respond. And then it IS sort of like a conversation. But one which is happening much later than my first thoughts on the topic. Thoughts you have bought and then read and then commented on in my DMs, maybe years later.

Again, no drugs were consumed in the writing of this chapter, but some supplements were. I take a little concoction of vitamins every day (when I remember). I always feel that it gives me a free pass to have a doughnut, or a plate of creamy pasta, or three gin and tonics, without worrying as much as I would normally. I did a lot of research on what sort of vitamins and supplements would do the best job. You'd like to hear what they are? Well, OK ...

I started with the standard:

Multivitamin – A go-to for anyone who knows sod-all but wants a generic, 'Great, I've at least got quite a few different vitamins and minerals inside me so the lack of my five-a-day in fruit and veg is actually fine' kind of a boost.

Then came:

Mushroom Complex – Now I'm not entirely sure what this does, but I remember seeing it on a friend's social media page almost 10 years ago and completely buying into the few words she wrote. After googling it myself and reading about half a paragraph on it, I discovered that in fact six different types of dried mushrooms put into one thing can cure ... um, loads of sh*t. Basically, I was sold on it and I had two packets in my basket on Amazon before Adam had a chance to say, 'Wait, look, they're £20 f*cking quid each.'

OK, so this natural mushroom blend basically says if you take this, you're ultimately invincible. Well, not exactly, but it's supposed to help with immune support, brain and nervous system function; it's an antioxidant and anti-inflammatory and helps boost energy levels. I've just seen there's a documentary proving the effects of mushrooms and many different ones at that. I add it to our watchlist on Netflix.

That night, Adam spots it: 'Seriously, are you kidding?! A documentary on mushrooms? Where has this come from? Do you think this mushroom thing might be an unhealthy obsession?'

'No. And if you actually watch this documentary with me, you'll realise why it's a very healthy one.'

Milk Thistle – Widely known to help liver function and repair the liver, as well as other health benefits. How did I come to discover this stuff? Let me tell you. In my early twenties, I got Hepatitis A from shellfish, and a private doctor on Sloane Street told me that when he had contracted Hep A when he was 17 he took milk thistle. It's meant to help repair your liver by up to a third quicker than if you didn't take it.

That's right, as an out-of-work actress, working in a bar for £200 a week and renting a crappy room in a flat above a shop, I was casually spending hundreds of pounds on a visit to the doctor in one of the most expensive areas of London. No, I wasn't. My ex was a baron and his father told me to go to his doctor to get diagnosed, as my then doctor had taken one look at my yellow eyes and asked if I had 'been overdoing it a bit recently?' I had, but not any more than anyone else in their twenties during the festive season and certainly not enough to look like an alien. Anyway, I took it religiously, every day, as well as doing the norm of cutting out anything which makes your liver work hard, such as fats, oils and alcohol.

When I went back to the doctor for a check-up a few weeks later, he said it was the fastest recovery of Hepatitis A he had ever seen. And he was no spring chicken. That was it – I was destined to spend the rest of my life buying milk thistle on a repeat Amazon purchase. And I have. Much to the detriment of my bank account.

LivPro XL – I bought these by accident. Well, almost. I went on to Amazon to buy milk thistle and when it was sold out, these popped up as an alternative suggestion. I've never seen so many incredible reviews of people having complete turnarounds from fatty liver and liver disease to normal function. They have amazing other health benefits too, with natural ingredients such as Turmeric, Acai, Black Aged Garlic, Ginger Root, L-Glutamine, Folic Acid, Vitamins C, B and D and Choline. I mean, what's not to like? I had a liver and kidney test recently due to blood pressure and everything was normal, so effectively I didn't NEED to buy these. But I will still continue to pay through the nose to take them, mostly out of sheer paranoia.

Juice Plus+ Essentials Fruit and Vegetable and Berry Blend Capsules – We all know the health benefits of fruit and veg and I recently saw a news segment on *BBC Breakfast* where a doctor was talking about the health benefits of eating 10 portions a day (dried, frozen, canned, whatever). He said that studies from the last 10 years have proven that eating those 10 portions in whatever form can reduce your risk of eight different cancers by 50 per cent and if there was a pill we could take to do that, we all would. What, like a pill with a few of those portions of dried fruit and veg in an easy-to-swallow capsule? OK then.

That's it. NB: I'm not being sponsored by any vitamin or supplement. Many thanks.*

Whenever a friend comes to stay and I take my supplements, I always offer them some too. Almost like a going-away gift, or like I'm giving them a 'Thanks for coming' party bag or a 'Sorry I ruined your liver with that party last night, let me try to help rectify that' present. So, one time, in the summer of 2019 my friend Becs visited for the day and night from Berkshire (yes, the very Becs of bowling party fame; *see also* page 98). We had a BBQ and the kids were playing in the garden and in the paddling pool. The prosecco and 'good old times chats' were flowing. We put the kids to bed and had a few more drinks together, singing along to our favourite songs from our London days by asking Google, often over each other, to play the next one as soon as we thought of it – you know, standard 'drunk old friends' stuff.

The next day was another beautiful day so we decided to go out for lunch in a pub beer garden en route to where Becs would be heading afterwards. We had some great food and a Pimm's each; we said goodbye and she was on her way. A few hours later, she texted me saying, 'FFS,

---

* No, really. I am not being sponsored by any pharmaceutical company. All the vitamins and the benefits discussed in this chapter are based on my experiences alone and are illustrated for information purposes only. All individuals react differently to medication. You should seek professional advice from your GP before starting any new medication.

mate. I've been in the biggest panic all day. At the pub, when I went to the loo for a wee, I turned around to flush and got the shock of my life. I started sweating with worry. The loo roll and bowl of the loo were luminous yellow. Bright luminous. I mean, radioactive. I've never seen anything like it. I'll send you the photo I took if my hands would stop sweating so I could scroll through them. Mate, I'm going to die. All my lifestyle choices. My excessive drinking. It's now f*cked me. My liver can't take it anymore. It's not even just a bit yellow or brownish. It's F*CKING LUMINOUS. I've drunk about seven pints of water since getting home and it's still f*cking luminous.'

I was in such hysterics texting her back. I couldn't see, my eyes were full of water through crying at how dramatic this seemed to her when I knew there was a simple explanation.

I typed, 'Mate, you took a multivitamin this morning. It always does that to your wee.'

Almost immediately, she replied: 'You're kidding. Are you having me on. Really? Sh*t.'

She then said she had been googling 'bright yellow wee' and should have googled 'luminous wee' as now some sort of chart had come up with a sort of Litmus-style variations of yellows, saying what each one might be down to. She could now see it had vitamins and supplements as one of those reasons.

I was still bent double with laughter.

'Thanks, mate. Might have a glass of champers to celebrate,' she wrote.

'W' IS FOR 'WANKY RESTAURANTS' ...

The movie's release is nearly upon us and we take Chris, the director (in case you forgot), out for dinner. Look, I say 'we' are taking him out, but WE won't actually be doing anything of the sort. We'll be meeting him at the restaurant, eating and drinking like kings and then allowing the restaurant to cover the bill. I'll explain, because I sound a bit like an arrogant, presumptuous tw*t. Over lockdown, I did an advert for a gorgeous restaurant in London to promote their steak and wine delivery service while their doors had to remain closed. Now that they're open again and as a thank you, they have invited me and Adam to dine on them. Not actually ON them. That would be weird and highly inappropriate. So now we're taking Chris as well, to a very expensive restaurant in our capital city to say thank you for giving me a role in the film. But we won't be paying for him either. So effectively, the restaurant will be saying thank you to him for giving me a part in the film. Chris's birthday also happened to be yesterday. How do I know this? Because just before filming the movie, I decided to do some very laid-back, superficial stalking of Chris online. And after three hours of scouring the internet, I just happened across his date of birth. It was a nice surprise that the meal coincided almost exactly with his actual birthday as this could be a double celebration of the movie and his birthday. I'm only joking about stalking him online for three hours – it was more like two and a half.

We arrive at the restaurant and I give my surname: Batten.

They say, 'I'm sorry, we don't seem to have that name down here. Is it definitely for 6 p.m.?'

Well, this is rather embarrassing.

'Yes, 6 p.m. Maybe it's under Clara Batten, or just Clara.'

I peer over the screen to look down at the list below 6 p.m. Even upside down I can see what most social media people would consider a bit of a nightmare: their surname changed to the online platform they most often use.

'Oh look, that's me: "Clara TikTok".' I couldn't help but smile. And Chris found it way funnier than he probably should have.

'And I'm Chris Instagram and this is Adam Facebook.'

I laughed out loud.

'She does actually know my name, guys. She sent me a load of steak and wine addressed to my actual name. She DID. Anyway, I rather like Clara TikTok. It has a ring to it, a really sh*t ring to it.'

We were shown to our table and we handed Chris a birthday card and a bottle of bloody nice champagne as a thank you and for his birthday. You can go one of two ways when buying champagne. Go with a really well-known good one, like Laurent-Perrier or Veuve Clicquot, or choose one that's not so well known but has a great bottle, good name but the reason the person receiving it doesn't recognise the name is because it could easily be way more expensive than the recognised brands. In this case, it was neither of those things: it was a bloody impressive bottle, beautiful name and pretty cheap. Sorted.

'Have you ever tried this, Chris? It's really stunning.' I have zero idea but it definitely has the word 'champagne' on the outside and I'm almost positive you're not going to get many sh*t champagnes. My best friend Rob is a brand ambassador for a wine company and would be so proud of my knowledge and chat right now.

'I haven't, I don't think. Excuse me, may we put this on ice? I'd like to share this with my friends.'

He thinks we're his friends? Low standards on his part.

He told us that while he is in England, he is staying solo in an apartment in King's Cross and didn't fancy drinking a bottle of champagne chilling on his own one night watching Netflix and would rather share it tonight with people he likes. Is he mad?! That's my ideal evening right there.

But my slight worry now though is that we might see his actual reaction to a pretty average champagne. I'm kidding – he's not that pretentious.

'Well, I think to start, it has to be the Oysters and Fillet of Beef Carpaccio with Shaved Black Truffle.'

Oh, maybe he is.

He's not, promise.

Anyway, I don't go to many top restaurants but I'm pretty sure drinking champagne that you've brought yourself and asking the staff to chill it for you isn't the 'done thing'. Or maybe top restaurants are so sympathetic to the fact that people are spending a lot of money that they are just very kind to their customers. But hang on, we're not even paying so ... wait, I get it now.

We start on some chilli margaritas, which Chris ordered without even looking at the menu. Hold on, he's sounding more pretentious by the minute. I had never heard of such a concoction before but they were delicious. I've only ever had chilli in gin and tonics but chilli in margaritas is another level. I wonder whether three minutes into sitting down is too early to ask Chris if he has anything else going on film or TV commercial-wise. It turns out I don't think it is, as I blurt out, 'So, Chris, got any new projects in the pipeline? Any films coming up? Anything you might need any female actors to audition for?'

'Not since the last time you asked me yesterday. Still just the same film, probably set in Ireland, but maybe not even for a couple of years yet.'

I let him know that I can get away with my Southern Irish accent but probably not my Northern Irish accent. It's a good job I let him know as obviously that was probably going to be the only sticking point as to why I may not get a part in it.

'Actually, the part that springs to mind if you were to audition, I would want you to play it in your normal accent anyway. By the way, have you started looking for an agent yet?' I'm sure he only asks me about agents because then everything would have to start going through them and I wouldn't be 'able' to pester him so much directly. 'Well, if you haven't, maybe wait until the film comes out and you can show them some good stuff. And go for a top gun. A big'un. You can.'

Wow. Turns out he's alright with me hounding him after all. At least that's what I took from that.

'OK, can I have that in writing?'

I order fillet steak and the men – I mean lads, I mean boys – order a tomahawk steak (the restaurant's recommendation). This is essentially a rib-eye steak but a bloody massive one with at least a five-inch rib bone still in it.

This is the largest, most expensive steak on the menu and it's the first one they recommended, so maybe they're just very nice at this restaurant? Not as expensive as Salt Bae's restaurants, mind. Have you heard about this person? He has basically created a ridiculously ostentatious and overpriced chain of restaurants which, from the many reviews I have read, actually produces below par food. I mean fair play to him. He has quite literally taken the p*ss out of the people he targets. Those who 'want to be seen in certain places', who don't care so much for quality as the status or glamour that might come from the talk of being in such a place and he seems to have nailed it.

Apparently, the hourly wage at his London restaurant is the same amount as it cost for a corn on the cob on his menu. Taking the p*ss out of customers who are willing to pay extortionate prices is one thing. Taking the p*ss out of your staff quite another. Oh sh*t, I've just looked it up: a corn on the cob is £14. I'll work for him.

It says it all when his Wikipedia describes him as a Turkish chef (and next) food entertainer, whose technique for preparing and seasoning meat became an internet meme in January 2017. Food entertainer comes before restaurateur.

What even is a food entertainer? Apparently, it's a person whose technique of seasoning meat became an internet meme, meaning they can now charge £850 for a steak. Even the best steak in the world is still a steak. It's from a cow, gold-leaf encrusted or not. Gold leaf actually tastes of nothing. 'One diner was furious when they got a £37,000 bill for four of them,' *The Sun* reports. And as if that wasn't barmy enough, evening bookings are completely full, so people are selling their reservations online for up to £250 a pop!

I read a hilarious review of Salt Bae's restaurant Nusr-Et in the *Guardian*. Reviewer Jay Rayner compared it to one of my go-to kebab haunts after a p*ssed night out when I lived in Parsons Green for circa 10 years, Kebab Kid. (To be honest, this isn't your regular kebab place. It's proper strips of seasoned meat layered every morning to create a succulent, delicious shawarma. I just WISH they served garlic sauce with it. The only thing missing in mine and so many other minds.) But if you ever get to visit this place, GET ONE. I'm not on commission. This isn't a pretentious kebab place, it's just bloody great.

What made me laugh about Jay Rayner's *Guardian* piece is that he decides to take his kebab and set up a table outside Nusr-Et, at which to eat his food. He says, 'A Sunday lunchtime and I am sitting outside a restaurant in London's Knightsbridge famed for serving a £1,450 steak, eating an £8.50 kebab. I have brought my own table, chair and chequered tablecloth. It's a ludicrous gesture, but then the Nusr-Et Steakhouse is a ludicrous restaurant, and one stupid turn deserves another. Still, I'm certain that I am eating better than all the customers through the huge wooden doors behind me, spaffing their sticky largesse over gold-leaf wrapped steaks. Because my lamb shawarma comes from the legendary Kebab Kid in Parsons Green, and very nice it is, too.'

I want to buy that man a drink.

Thankfully, the food at Smith & Wollensky London was incredible. Plus, they very kindly gave Chris the biggest slice of birthday cake I have ever seen, which obviously, by the look of excitement on his silly little face, took him back to his childhood. Or at least I hope so, otherwise he's just bloody immature.

Anyway, I'm annoyed I've probably given Salt Bae a bit too much airtime. Either way, I don't think myself, or that *Guardian* fella Jay, will be invited to his restaurant any time soon. But I'm also not sure we're going to lose too much sleep over it, either.

*   *   *

It's the morning after the night before and I'm not feeling my best. I'm not sure why the mixture of chilli margaritas, champagne, red wine and espresso martinis hasn't made me feel on top of the world. Now I understand that *Withnail and I* quote, because I actually DO feel like a pig sh*t in my head. I've downed three pints of water and it still feels exactly the same. I sift through the medicine drawer looking for some paracetamol. Or ibuprofen. Anything. Oh good, two empty packs which have been put back in the drawer to get anyone with a throbbing head excited then nicely let down. I can't carry on today like this. Out of the corner of my eye, I spot a purple bottle. I know what that is: Calpol. Calpol contains paracetamol. Paracetamol for ages two months to six years but I'm all over it. I must be allowed triple what the kids are, given my size. I pick up the bottle and, without a thought (don't try this at home), put it straight to my mouth as if it's a bottle of Coke and glug three big gulps. At this point, I don't know whether to be disgusted with myself or extremely proud of my innovation.

'X' IS FOR 'XYLOPHONE' ...

When someone asks what word begins with 'X', it is always xylophone. There is no other word beginning with 'X' and even if there was no one knows of it, because 'X' is only ever for xylophone, which should actually begin with 'Z'. Sodding phonics. But weirdly, this time, and probably for the first time in history, the xylophone is actually relevant to the story.

Our neighbours kindly said Adam and I could host our 40th birthday party – marquee and all – in their field, which adjoins our garden. As our garden is filled with kid paraphernalia, we were quick to accept. We were concerned that the wire fence and stinging nettles separating our garden and their field might be a hindrance to guests because they would have to climb over it all in their party frocks, but at least they would gain numerous free stings up their legs along the way, so every cloud ... After a long discussion, it seemed only right to cut the nettles away, buy a proper solid wooden gate and pay for a professional to come and install it on the boundary, which I was delighted with as it ended up costing more than the whole party.

On Party Day, 14 August, the weather was on our side. We erected the marquee the day before and the chef arrived with his butcher's burgers, sausages and marinated chicken and set up the BBQ. I'm busy in the kitchen with my sister-in-law VJ, because every BBQ needs at least seven different salads and my brother Ben and Adam are filling a full-size canoe with bottles of booze. Yes, you read that right: we thought stashing the bottles in a canoe full of ice would look quite cool and had nothing else big enough to keep all the bottles cool in. Absolutely nothing else other than a canoe.

I realise, in the midst of all the kitchen chaos, that half the salads aren't gluten-free: there's pasta in one, noodles in another and croutons in a third. So, in fact, most of them aren't really salads at all. Anyway, there's no way that gluten-intolerant people can only have access to four salads. I must think fast.

'Quinoa!' I shout, with the pronunciation 'qui-no-a', as I storm into the kitchen.

'Sorry? What's that?' VJ asks.

'That stuff that's a bit like couscous but gluten-free.'

'Ah, kee-noi …' I'm corrected by my 10-year-old niece, Isla, who is half-listening while she casually pours herself an orange juice.

'Yes, that stuff. I've never cooked it before in my life, but I reckon if I roast some vegetables which I don't have, chuck those in the quinoa which I have not yet bought, add some soy sauce ...'

'Soy sauce isn't gluten-free,' my eight-year-old nephew, George, pipes up.

Seriously? I mean what are these two, child prodigies?

'Remember, Mum can't eat gluten.'

Oh, yes.

VJ follows with, 'Seriously, Ra, we don't need quinoa. You've got so many dishes, without the quinoa. Plus, going out to get quinoa will waste time. Forget the quinoa.'

'OK. So long as you stop saying quinoa.'

As everyone arrives, we do our best to show the kids that our garden is 'their area' and the field next door is more the grown-up area. They have the blow-up water park, trampoline and zip wire, and are loving it. The parents are getting some respite and, for a while, things are pretty civilised. Sunny weather, the clinking of glasses, food aplenty, laughter and the band is playing chilled, folky music. But as evening falls, the vibe quickly descends into a middle-class rave. It's as if we've missed three hours somewhere. There's disco lights in the marquee, live classic pop and rock songs being played, the adults getting merry (plastered), dancing around fire pits (not in a weird cult way, more of an 'I'm cold, I could do with warming up' kind of way).

'Are you warm enough?' I ask my brother, Ben.

'Warm enough? No. I think only the right-hand side of my face has got third-degree burns. Hang on, let me change sides. Yep, there it is. Don't worry, warming up now.'

I decide the best thing to do at this point, given my love of singing, is to ask the band if they could play a few songs so I could sing using their lead singer's mic. Ben reminds me that this isn't karaoke as I try to drag him up with me to sing the harmonies. I sing three or four songs. I sound brilliant. I'm getting a few words wrong, even though I have the lyrics in front of me on my phone. In my defence, the words are very hard to read: they are either extremely small, or I suddenly need a very severe optician's appoint-ment, or lyrics.com have weirdly written all the lyrics twice, ever so slightly overlapping each other.

Cressy sees me up there and runs to the house to get something, anything, to join in. She rushes out with a xylophone (*see?*), but not a grown-up xylophone which has real notes on it, a toy one she has had since she was two, which hardly makes a noise but when it does every 'note' sounds exactly the same. She's in her element, so I ask for a mic to be nearer her, which wasn't necessary in the slight-est. I beckon my best friend Pip up to sing with me. 'Hotel California' is one of our classic karaoke duets from our late teens and we're going to nail it. I mime the words 'film it' to my other best mate Rob and he takes out his phone enthusiastically. Rather *too* enthusiastically, as if this might be more 'comedy gold' than Spandau Ballet singing 'Gold'. At the end of the song, Pip and I give each other a praising hug, give Cressy, who is waving her xylophone in the air to the whoops and cheers of our friends, a congratulatory squeeze and walk off the makeshift stage extremely chuffed with ourselves.

One of the local village people (oh, how I wish I meant the band) rushes over to me and says, 'That was brilliant.'

'Thanks! I really love singing,' I say proudly.

'No, seriously, I took loads of videos. Look, they're hilarious. You had us in hysterics.'

'Huh?'

She shows me a snippet of one of the songs. This can't be me. She must have used a comedy voice tuning app in the last 45 seconds to f*ck with me. How can you actually sound like you're slurring your words while singing? Isn't that what singing is? But this is definitely slurring and stuttering and singing, well, *slightly* out of tune. OK, being described as a drowning cat would have been a compliment at this point. Imagine what it will sound like when I'm sober. Sh*t. And with that, I hear a scream, followed by plenty of raucous laughter: our friends Neil and Sarah have fallen off the hay bales onto a pile of sticks assembled dangerously close to the bonfire.

'Do you reckon we could leave our car at yours, so we can get a cab?' Sarah asks, still lying on top of Neil, who has two twigs jutting out from his hair, not dissimilar to the Andorians in *Star Trek*.

'Yeah, sure. You can pick up the *Starship Enterprise* tomorrow.'

*　　*　　*

I won't bore you with another terrible hangover story but, suffice to say, the morning after the party was BRUTAL. How did I get through it? With another of my guilty pleasures: reality TV, and specifically the dating kind.

I either get really hooked or really bored very quickly but at least you know at the start if it's going to be a good 'un or a bad 'un. *Love Island* is one that I can't not watch. Like a car crash that you don't want to look at but can't help yourself, it has become a global phenomenon around the world, so at least I'm not the only one.

The premise, for those of you who have been living under a rock, is that 10 singles – five men and five women – are shipped off to a villa somewhere sunny and spurred on by a lack of internet and small double beds they have to share with strangers, they try to find true love. What could go wrong? When they 'couple up', they have to share a bed together, whether romantically involved or not. But undoubtedly, if they ARE romantically involved, their ability to hold off on doing anything sexual despite sharing a bedroom with eight to 12 others is limited. They're like rottweilers on heat but, luckily, they hide it well by covering their heads with their duvets, rendering the mysterious up and down movements and panting completely invisible and silent to those watching on their TV screens.

Oh, and also behind the scenes are a bunch of potential islanders, sometimes even contestants' exes, waiting on standby to be sent in during the course of the season, normally as others are voted out either by their fellow contestants or us the public. I say 'us'. Of course I've never voted. I never get that into it. Like, never. Really, I don't. Maybe just the free vote on the app.

So that's *Love Island* in a nutshell. Not really a nutshell, maybe that's *Love Island* in a huge, flourishing acorn tree. But seriously, it's on another level in comparison to the very tame and scripted *Blind Date* – the only dating show on TV when I was growing up.

My dating show obsession doesn't stop there, oh no. I'm also a fan of *Married at First Sight*, which is like *Love Island* but with older contestants. And by 'older', I mean mainly in their thirties. And the stakes are much higher as they're getting married to someone they've never met before and the first time they see them is at the altar. Now this isn't as big as *Love Island*, granted, but it's bloody brilliant and addictive.

A word of advice: don't bother with the British version unless they've recently taken a leaf out of the Australians' increasingly salacious and dramatic book.

Though reality TV has my heart, I'm also partial to a bit of true crime. Now I'm not sure about anyone else, but when I watched *Making a Murderer*, there is absolutely no way the Wisconsin PD, LA PD or any other PD would not hire me after the stuff I managed to write down while solving that murder. I have no shame in admitting I was the best armchair detective of 2015. It also coincided with a time of my life when I was in between jobs and, although I didn't watch this series during the day without Adam, I may or may not have been a tad obsessed with the Crime & Investigation channel. Of course, I would only watch it while eating lunch. Otherwise, I was searching for jobs … Definitely searching for jobs.

Adam, who worked just eight minutes from our flat at the time, would come back for lunch sometimes. On two consecutive days he walked in at the exact moment the advert breaks came on. Day 1, it flashed up *Wives with Knives*. He laughed and said, 'Bloody hell, I only came back for a sandwich.' On the second day he walked in and, as I tried to grab the remote to put the TV on standby, up popped *Snapped: Women Who Kill* – 'F*cking hell. Do I have anything to worry about?' he said. On the third day he walked in and the TV was paused on a McDonald's advert. 'Thank God,' he muttered to himself. As I made my way back from the loo, he had already pressed play while getting leftovers out from the fridge. He sat down while he waited for the microwave to ping and across the TV in big red letters were the words *The Devil You Know*.

'My food is almost done, then I'll leave you to it, you psychopath.'

LIFE LESSON
ACCORDING TO CLARA BATTEN: 11

NEVER UTTER THE WORDS 'ONE MORE EPISODE' ABOUT ANYTHING.

This will ultimately mean you binge-watch the entire series that very night and you will have absolutely no control over it.

'Y' IS FOR 'YOGA' ...

We're going on our first holiday in two years, to Tenerife for a little early winter sun. We booked it last-minute, two days ago. We're bloody crazy, I know. Talk about living life on the edge.

Now, however much we attempt to change the type of holiday we go on, we always resort to the trusted 'All Inclusive'. It's about £150 more per person for the week, but it means we don't stress about how much the kids do (or don't) eat and we can all stuff our faces with eggs, sausages, waffles, pancakes, pastries, cheese, cold meats and doughnuts – and that's just breakfast. The entertainment is cheesy but reliable, the kids are taken off our hands for an hour of mini-disco in the evenings and having a Buck's Fizz at 10 a.m. is not frowned upon. Bliss.

On arrival I have the best intentions. I will not put on a stone in one week but I will enjoy myself. I shall fill up at the salad bar at any mealtime before venturing on to the hot-plate stations. I'll get involved in any sports and physical activities on offer and will only have one alcoholic drink before midday three times in the week.

Although all the activities on this holiday are included, some have limited space and require advance registration. The water aerobics is a free-for-all, but the terrace sunrise and sunset yoga sessions are taken very seriously. To be honest, neither of these times are ideal for me. I don't want to wake up before my children and maybe with a slight hangover. Also, I don't want to be in my sportswear, getting sweaty as the sun is going down while everyone else is dressed up for the evening, having Sex on the Beach – and also drinking the odd cocktail.

I sign up for sunrise. Well, that was a mistake.

Somehow I make it to the first session on the morning of Day 2 of being in Tenerife, even after a rather bustling first night of meeting new people and drinking 'free' drinks. But I feel more tired than when I was up for two days in an induced labour. I yawn four times consecutively as I join the group on the terrace.

'Sorry I'm a few minutes late but, to be honest, I'm very proud to have even got up this early. Don't think I've ever seen the sunrise on holiday. I'm absolutely exhausted.'

'Sunrise is at 8 a.m.'

Halfway through the yoga session, my phone rings. I apologise and ignore it. It rings again. I apologise once more and pick it up: it's my neighbour from back in England. It's 8 a.m. This is odd.

'Clara, there's someone banging on our door, shouting, "When was the Great Fire of London?" She seems a bit mad. But she says she's your cleaner and needs to get in because your alarm is going off.'

'Oh yes, sorry, this is the code to our gates. She must have forgotten her key. So sorry. A bit of trivia for you, though: do you know when the Great Fire of London was?' I turn around to everyone in the yoga class standing still, looking at me.

'Well, yes, but OK ...' I hear her shout out of her window 'Ten sixty-six.'

'No. You see loads of people get those mixed up. That was the Battle of Hastings. It's literally the only thing I remember from history lessons and that's only because I made it my gate code.

'Sh*t. I mean 1666. F*ck me, this is not what I expected to be doing at 8.05 a.m. on a Wednesday morning.'

'Thanks, mate. Sorry. Got to get back to yoga.' I turn back to the class: 'As you were ...'

The rest of the class was filled with almost impossible moves and stances I can only think must have been taken from the Kama Sutra. I get back to the hotel room, red-faced, sweaty and limping.

Adam welcomes me with, 'Jesus, look at the state of you! You were doing yoga, not running a half marathon.'

And even though I was very capable and getting up early was probably going to do me the world of good, I very selflessly decided to give my yoga slot away for the rest of the week.

That night, in my summer dress, newly showered, make-up done, cocktail in hand, watching the yoga fanatics on that terrace, I felt very smug. Even though they probably weren't fanatics and were just able to do 45 minutes of what was now looking, from the outside, like quite simple stretching. We grab another drink and agree to head to dinner after this one so the kids can be in time for their little disco. Monty is desperate for his monster truck he left in the hotel room so I head up there with him to get it. On our way back down, we bump into a couple we have been talking to earlier by the pool and we get into the lift together. Once we leave the lift the woman says, 'Didn't you have your son with you just now?'

Sh*t. He's like a whippet. He was definitely in the lift with us. Or was he?

I frantically go back into the lift, three times in total, as if he might magically appear in the two-square-metre area he was not in the first time I looked. I run up the stairs in case he decided he wanted to walk down. Not there. He must have scooted past us when leaving the lift and back to Daddy. I jog, in only one-inch heels, but still manage to do it in the most unladylike, awkward fashion, back to our table and ask if Monty is with them.

'Can you see him here?' Adam asks while sitting, just with Cressy, at a table for four.

We spend the next 15 minutes going to reception, asking the lifeguards, rushing around every section of the hotel we have not been to. He is nowhere to be seen. The staff start to check CCTV. I try one last thing: our room is on the fourth floor and you have to walk down two different corridors outside and inside the building in order to get to it. It's like a maze, and if you get in the wrong lift you end up in a completely different area of the hotel altogether. I've never run so quickly. I start to think maybe that yoga session has done something for me after all, or perhaps it's just the adrenaline of losing a three-year-old. As I turn the corner of the final corridor, I see Monty sitting outside our hotel room on the floor, holding his monster truck in his lap. I run up to him, saying, 'Monty darling, I didn't know where you were, sweetheart.'

'I just here. I didn't know where you were so I came back to our room.'

At this point, I'm pretty sure my three-year-old is more worldly than me. And I know I'll be calling on his weird satellite navigation brain in a couple of hours when we head back to the room for bed.

Luckily, the rest of the week wasn't quite so eventful as the first 24 hours. Although Cressy, at four, swam her first width of the pool in the deep end unaided, the two kids learnt the 'Island Dance' by Night 2, Monty went down the big kid slide 32 times in one day, the hotel mascot was still as scary on Day 7 as on Day 1, Adam acquired a bottle of something rank by winning a Butlins-style 'Macho Man' competition, which was less like two men having an arm wrestle to 'Eye of the Tiger' and more like two boys dressing up as Tina Turner and miming to 'Simply the Best' while doing a dance-off, and I set my alarm twice to pretend I was watching the sunrise but really I was just basking in the glory of relief that I was having a croissant and a Buck's Fizz, watching the morning struggles of those attempting a Downward Dog.

*   *   *

Back home, and Adam and I have had a random invitation. Not a physical invitation through the post, a DM. Of course. Because apparently this is just how people communicate nowadays. It's from Carrie Johnson, the then Prime Minister Boris's wife. She says that her family have been really enjoying my videos (I hope she doesn't mean her toddler and baby, given my content) and that if it's not too short notice, would we be available to come to Chequers for dinner that Friday? Adam can't quite believe his ears when I read this out to him, but still checks his diary, just in case we have more on than just our usual Friday 'Netflix and chill'. Not in that way, I mean actually watch a crime documentary and be in bed latest by 10 p.m. to scroll the news.

'All good, is it? You don't have darts booked in with a couple of mates at the local? So, shall I accept the invitation to dine with the Prime Minister and his wife at their country estate, or shall I postpone?' We figured that – whatever your political views – they'd be pretty bloody good craic to hang out with, so accept.

Three days later, and with Nana babysitting, we drive the two hours to the quaint country pub we have booked a room at for the night. As we order a sharpener drink to take to the room while we get ready, Adam reminds me we have to book a cab to Chequers itself.

I call a local cab company.

'Hello, I don't know what time we need to order a cab for as I'm not sure how long it takes to get there from here. But we need to be at Chequers for 7.30 p.m. and we're at the Red Lion in Wendover. Do you know how long that will take, please?'

'Is that the Chequers in the High Street, love?'

'Um, no. Er, sorry, this is going to sound really weird. But it's Chequers, as in the Prime Minister's country residence. I know, it's a bit silly, really.' Not sure why I was suddenly sounding like a character from *Four Weddings and a Funeral*. (Maybe because, as you might have surmised, I have a small Richard Curtis obsession. No need to get concerned yet, Richard.)

'Oh gosh, right, um, *that* Chequers,' the *Four Weddings'* thing was rubbing off on her. 'Well, that's only five minutes away but we will pick you up at 7.15 p.m. to make sure you're not late.'

'Thank you, but I think it's almost ruder to be early, don't you think? I mean, I hate it when people are early to something I've invited them to. What if they're not ready?'

'Ah, yes. But it IS Friday night and there will be a little more traffic than normal. Maybe we can pull over near there and wait if you DO get there early?'

'Good idea. Won't that clock up the meter though, sitting nearby for 10 minutes? Either way, I definitely owe you some business, given the amount of time I have clogged up your line for talking about this. See you at 7.15 p.m. Thank you.'

As I get off the phone, Adam is sitting in the armchair in the corner of the room, Cuba Libre in hand, shaking his head slowly.

'I know, I know, but I needed to be thorough. It's rude to be early.'

'No, it's not that. Just listening to that conversation out loud, it *does* sound ridiculous. The "going to Boris and Carrie's for dinner" part. I know you've messaged each other a few times, but you've not spoken to her on the phone, she has a private Instagram account which is not verified and she didn't ask us to bring any ID to one of the most security-protected establishments in the world. Are you sure you're not being trolled?'

'Well, now you say it like that ...'

I was doubting everything now, but after a couple of stiff drinks we were well on our way to a dinner we blatantly weren't invited to.

En route, I get a text message from Philly, the writer

friend of mine: 'Mate, wouldn't Boris make a brilliant father to Jeremy [our main character] in the sitcom? You HAVE to ask him.'

'Yeah, I'll certainly try. I'll shout it down the massive driveway as we're being manhandled off the premises.'

* * *

Three armed policemen approach the car as we pull up to the intercom and gate at the end of the driveway. We open the window to the cab and I lean across Adam to talk to them.

'Hello, we're here to see the Johnsons for dinner, whether they like it or not. Ha!' Now is not the time to be joking around.

'Are you their guests for this evening?'

'Yes?' I say, doubting myself. 'I mean, we think so? *Are* we?'

At this point Adam has his elbow on the window, head in his hand.

'What are your names?'

'Clara and Adam Batten.'

'ID?'

'Yep, luckily for you. And us. We brought our passports along, even though they didn't ask us to bring any. And they've never even met us, we just follow each other on social media.'

Shut up, Clara.

While the policeman looks through our passports for

longer than it takes at immigration, the cab driver turns to us in the back and, without moving his lips, whispers, 'What is this place?'

'The Prime Minister sometimes stays here when he's not at No. 10.'

'OK, out you get,' one policeman orders.

I knew it: we're about to be arrested. Why did we do this? So stupid. And bloody pathetic.

He continues, 'The housekeeper is driving down to pick you up.'

'Oh great, so our names are on the door?'

'Well, not like at a nightclub, but yes.'

Five minutes later, we are in a Fiat or something just as down-to-earth, on our way up what seemed a mile-long driveway, excited that we weren't about to spend the night in a prison cell, but have supper in the rose garden of the Prime Minister's country house.

They greeted us with big affable smiles at the front door and immediately I went in for the hug as Boris put out his hand.

Great start.

'I'll take a hug!' Carrie exclaims and Boris follows with one too.

We walk through the vast, ancient rooms towards the gardens, while Boris tells us they have both had a couple of strong negronis as they were rather nervous about meeting us. This is the funniest thing I've ever heard. Nervous? *Them*? About meeting *us*?

I won't bore you with the ins and outs of the evening. Some things are probably best left private anyway. But they were warm and funny and easy to get on with. One of the first things I noticed is they treated their staff with decency, affection and gratitude. We had a tour of the (incredible) house, heard tales of the history and of parties there, had margaritas in the famous 'Long Room', an unexpected sleepover in 'Winston Churchill's' room (not all together, you weirdos!) and, amazingly, I have a voice note to my friend Philly from Boris, saying he 'would be very happy to play Jeremy's father in our up-and-coming sitcom'.

That's a verbal contract, right?

'Z' IS FOR 'ZERO MUM GUILT' ...
(Sort of)

QUOTES BY CRESSY

Cressy: 'I've been talking to Father Christmas tonight, Mummy. I said that I would like a box of slime and a robot that does absolutely everything for me. When I say "everything", Mummy, I mean "everything". I think that's OK for Father Christmas to get.'

It's the premiere for *A Christmas Number One* tonight. I'm thinking red carpet, ball gowns, the press, Odeon Cinema, Leicester Square ... I've got one thing right: it IS in Leicester Square. Well, sort of. It's in an independent cinema on a side street just off Leicester Square. And less ball gown, more whatever you want and not so much press and red carpet as me asking random passers-by if they can take a quick photo of us outside the cinema using my phone.

OK, so it's the cast and crew screening, but it's the first time we are all seeing the film so technically that is a premiere. I mean, what does 'premiere' even mean? It means first. So, although we may not have black tie and limousines, we are watching it for the first time, in an actual cinema, and I have just seen an email saying we no longer have to make our own way to the afterparty as they have arranged for a coach to pick us all up.

Who's laughing now?

I spot Chris, give him a hug and congratulate him.

I'm wearing a gold-sequined bomber jacket, gold animal print leggings and black boots with gold buckle. I'm not selling this look; I understand that, now I am typing it out. Chris is in an all-black suit, black shirt and a normal black tie.

'Jesus, Clara, you could have dressed up a bit! It's not a funeral,' he says.

We grab some cans of G&T from the bar and make our way in. As I sit in that cinema, looking up at the big screen, seeing my eight-foot head doing what it's always dreamed of doing, acting its little socks off, I felt quite emotional. No matter what age you are or how many kids you have had, you can still be a middle-aged actress with a few lines in a Christmas film and do am-dram in your village the rest of the time.

Never give up on your dreams.

The film was so much better than I expected – and I expected a lot after being on set and watching everything take shape. The atmosphere in the cinema was electric and I was having the time of my life. We all cheered at the big moments and the 'in jokes', we cracked up at the brilliantly delivered one-liners, we sang along to the cheesy songs and there was a standing ovation and cheering at the end.

One coach ride later, a wristband and a glass of prosecco down, and we were at the afterparty. Prosecco? That's basically white wine with bubbles so I decide to have one, maximum. But hold on, the gin and rum aren't free, so I switch back to the prosecco and try not to envisage what state I'll be in, in three hours' time.

After the most amazing night filled with live performances by Chris (he's the director, by the way) and the film's made-up boy band 5 Together, loads of dancing, masses of laughter, photos galore and a lot of reminiscing, I am on my two-hour cab journey heading out of the Big Smoke and towards home. I look out at the city lights and feel pensive. It may be the drink, but a tear rolls down my face. Like a cheesy film montage, all of the experiences I have had this year, culminating in tonight, race through my mind. I'm so very grateful for them all. I close my eyes, put my head against the window and smile.

The cab driver interrupts my reverie: 'Excuse me, lady, do you mind if we stop somewhere? I really need a p*ss.'

> ## QUOTES BY CRESSY
>
> The morning after the premiere, Cressy says: 'Mummy,
> I would love to act more and not just on your TikTok
> stuff. Can you ask Chris if I can be in *A Christmas
> Number Two*?'

I was on a post-premiere high when things got even better. Another DM. I'm beginning to like these a lot. An acting agent got in touch to tell me that she had watched the film and that it would be great to chat, asking if I currently have representation (again, can we all just assume I do not have an agent for anything). That is, until NOW! After a Zoom meeting with the agent, who turned out to be just as bonkers as me, it took little time (and not just because no other agents have approached me) for me to agree we would be the perfect match.

Maybe, just maybe, I might just act in more than my village pantomime in the future.

Now, I'm coming to the end of this book just as the film has been released and just before the Christmas school holidays start, and I'm going to enjoy every moment of these days with Cressy and Monty; give them every ounce of me and every possible Christmassy experience they deserve and, most importantly, family time. We'll eat cheese (mostly me), eat chocolate (at 9 a.m.), toast marshmallows (without ending up in the burns unit) and dance to Christmas songs. We'll play with monster trucks and dinosaurs and then Adam will have to let Monty have a turn. We'll do the phonics Cressy loves in the evenings and I'll keep my mouth shut about it and have a G&T while we're doing it, probably. We'll see Father Christmas, eat Bratwurst hot dogs, go to Winter Wonderland and go on the Santa steam train. And all while having zero 'mum guilt'. OK, *almost* zero.

Committing to writing a book when you have two young kids, school holidays, unpredictable illnesses, sleepless nights and unexpected family stuff has been a test, to say the least. I've probably written more words than I wrote in all my years at school. Now that may not be entirely true (don't @ me, I haven't done the maths), but it's been hard. Harder than I could have imagined when I said yes. It's been difficult, testing, cathartic, emotional but most of the time I have really enjoyed it. I have learnt. I have laughed. I have cried. And it's an experience I will never forget. It is also my biggest and proudest achievement to date (other than my two little treasures, I hasten to add) and one I hope the kids will realise means they can also do anything they want, however big.

This book has also been a companion to me during some pretty huge life shifts. I turned 40. There is that age-old saying that 'life begins at 40'; when I looked at my parents at 40, in my teens, all those years ago, I saw them as 'old', but now I know the aphorism is true. Don't get me wrong, I had a fulfilling life up until this point. I went to some great schools, had boyfriends who ran the full gamut from lovely to sh*t, endured a bit of trauma when my dad died too early, have travelled the world, learnt lessons in rubbish jobs with crapper-than-crap bosses and learnt other lessons in great jobs with amazing bosses. I've moved house more times than I can count on both hands. I've lived in one of the best capital cities of the world, met my soulmate, had and still do have the most incredible friends, birthed two children and I still think my best years are to come. I'm the most secure in my own skin, the most content, the most excited about the future, the most humbled by reality and wanting to do good and be better than I've ever been. I have fulfilled dreams this year I never thought imaginable, I've had the most unbelievable support from strangers on the internet I've never met. I've made people laugh and laughed so much myself, created memories in unusual circumstances with all of my family; danced, cried, been vulnerable, not been the best mum or wife at times, but also hopefully been the best at others. I've learnt a great deal, raised a lot of money for charities, acted in a film, written a script, written a goddamn f*cking book, but most importantly I've enjoyed life while doing it, even the challenging parts.

I hope you've enjoyed reading my words. I didn't want it to be another moany read about how hard it is to be a mum. Instead, I aimed for a smattering of humorous anec-dotes, a few (OK, one or two) thought-provoking moments and a whole lot of reality, but most of all I wanted you to smile. Maybe laugh. To feel seen. To care less about getting older and know that you can still do and be what and who you want to be. And to realise that most of us, deep down, are actually more similar than we might realise. Sorry, what a bloody insult that is to you.

Thank you all so much for coming on this bizarre journey with me and, well, 'taking a punt' as my publisher at HarperCollins said all those months ago. My only hope now is that my darling daddy up there can 'see' me and is proud. Who knew we'd end up here? Not me, but as I write these final lines, Philly and I are even talking about writing the film script of this book. Mostly because I want to be in another film and thought this might be the easiest way. Oh, and Richard Curtis ... if you haven't already taken out a restraining order on me, we'd gladly have you on board.

ACKNOWLEDGEMENTS

Thank you so much to Adam, my husband, for putting up with my silly antics, for getting involved in my sketches when I ask him to, and for having a 'normal job' supporting us all, while encouraging me in the pursuit of my dreams. He has been there physically and emotionally throughout this process (sorry about that); from listening when I've laughed and run a comedy sentence or two by him to providing a shoulder when I've needed the uplift and encouragement. Without your unwavering championing and cheering, I would not have written this book. I love you.

Thank you to my mother, Louise, for always believing in me and telling me I can do whatever I liked if it made me happy. For reminding me I don't need to do or be the norm, or follow the rat race, and that anything is possible. Without your support and my upbringing I wouldn't be this person and have the confidence to fulfil my ambitions. How lucky I am to have you.

Thank you to Ben, my eldest brother, who stepped up when our father passed away and helped me as a best friend and brother into adulthood, continuing to make me laugh and being a constant rock in my life.

And to Clive, my uncle. Thanks for being a friend first, uncle second and making us all laugh throughout the years.

Thank you to Oli Malcolm at HarperCollins for approaching me about a book, for believing in me, 'taking a punt' and holding my hand through the first few months of the process and being a mentor ever since, whether he liked it or not. I really, really appreciate you.

How to put into words my appreciation for my editor Cyan Turan at HarperCollins? I never knew how significant editors were until now. Thank you so much for being so approachable, for understanding my vision of what I wanted the book to be, for always being on the same page as me, for being a constant, loyal source of reassurance and great ideas and for your patience and enthusiasm. The time and energy you put in felt like it was 'your baby' as much as it was mine. And for that I thank you deeply.

Thank you to Katya Shipster at HarperCollins for your helpful input and always super advice.

Thank you to my agent, Alex at McLean-Williams Ltd, who I didn't have in my life when I agreed to this but has been a brilliant support since I signed with her, not just professionally but as a person I now class as a good friend I can approach about anything.

Thank you to Chris Cottam. I will never stop thanking you from the bottom of my heart. You saw something in me and you 'went with it', giving me a part in your film four weeks before shooting. You continue to make me laugh until I cry; you are kind, and so very decent. Thank you for still believing in me and putting me forward for roles. I'm genuinely honoured to call you a friend.

Thank you to the producers of *A Christmas Number One*: Robert, Camilla, Ruth and Debbie, who thought I was good enough to be in their Christmas movie, which made my whole year. So brilliant to now have you as friends. You might not feel so lucky when I hound you for the next part. See you on the next night out!

Thank you to the writers of the film, Keiron Self and Giles New. Without this script I would not have ended up going back to and giving my all, once again, to acting.

Thank you to three best friends, Rob, Pip and Laurie who have been there in person and on the other end of the phone these last few years when I've needed them most and made me laugh my head of when I've craved much needed escapism. Your unwavering support has never gone unnoticed.

Thank you so much to the brilliant Ruth Crafer, whose headshots captured my personality, almost too well.

Thanks to Amanda Holden, Simon Pegg and Phill Jupitus for your ongoing support. It means the world.

Thanks to James, Jo and Rich from Brennen and Brown distillery in Cheltenham for the *Gin & Phonics* gin!

Thank you to the legends who write hilarious memes and those who send them to me. Some of which have inspired content and life lessons along the way … memes give me life on a daily basis.

I mention in the book how really bad bosses can have a big impact on your life and how great ones can have an even bigger impact on you. When you get a good'un it makes you stop and notice. So thank you Josh, James L and Jack for being positive bosses in my life.

Thank you, Theo, for being my mate and brother growing up. We hope to see you soon.

And to my niece and nephews, Isla, George, Noah and Cash, for being the next generation of little legends I already know you are.

And lastly, thank you to my two children, Cressy and Monty, who make me laugh and make me want to be a better person daily. You are my biggest fans and you gave me the strength to continue writing this book, when I thought I may not succeed. You gave me more encouragement than you know and you gave me stories and memories to tell without realising it, with your barmy humour and unique characters. How exceptionally lucky I am to have you.